AN AERIAL VIEW OF THE

LOWCOUNTRY ALOFT

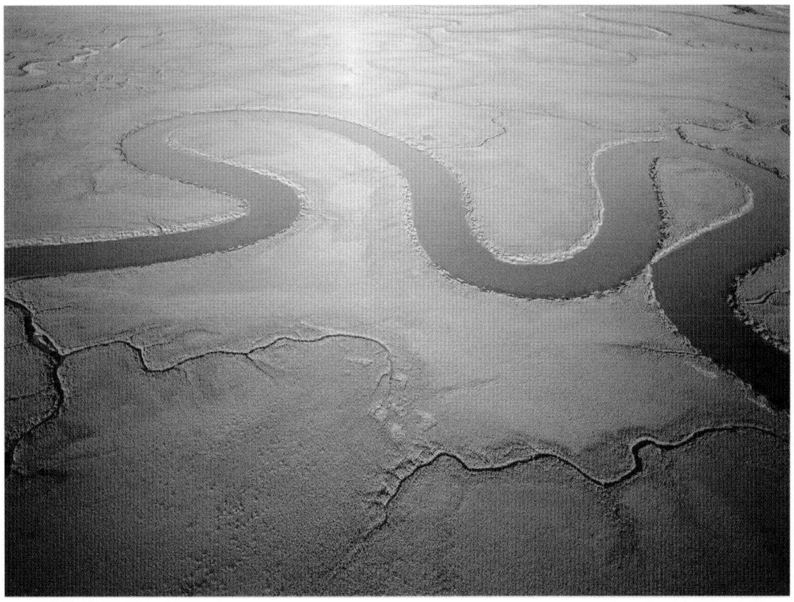

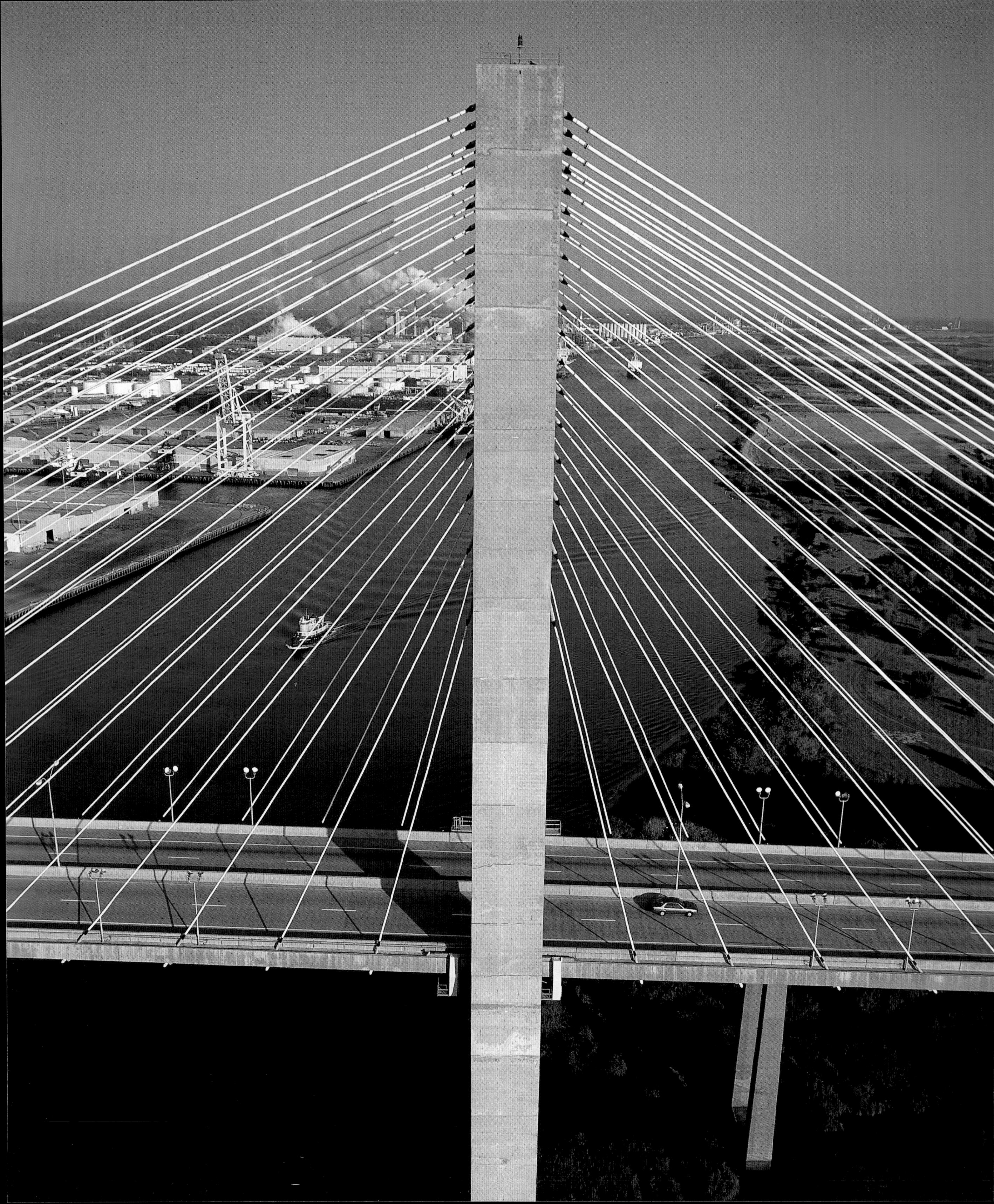

AN AERIAL VIEW OF THE

LOWCOUNTRY

PHOTOGRAPHY BY JASON HAWKES

ALOFT

John M. Trask, Jr.

Wyrick & Company
Charleston

This book is dedicated to everyone who shares a love and excitement for the good life that one can find in the land we call the Lowcountry – and especially to my wife Caroline, to our three sons and daughter and their spouses, and to our wonderful grandchildren. May each be blessed with a spirit of exploration in a never-ending discovery of the meaning of time and place.

- John M. Trask, Jr.

Published by Wyrick & Company
Post Office Box 89
Charleston, South Carolina 29402

Book design by Gil Shuler Graphic Design
Printed and bound in China by C&C Offset Printing Co.

Library of Congress Cataloging-in-Publication Data

Jacket Photo: Morris Island Lighthouse. Charleston.

Half Title Page Photo: Patterns of waterways. St. Helena Island.

Frontispiece Photo: Talmadge Memorial Bridge. Savannah.

PREFACE

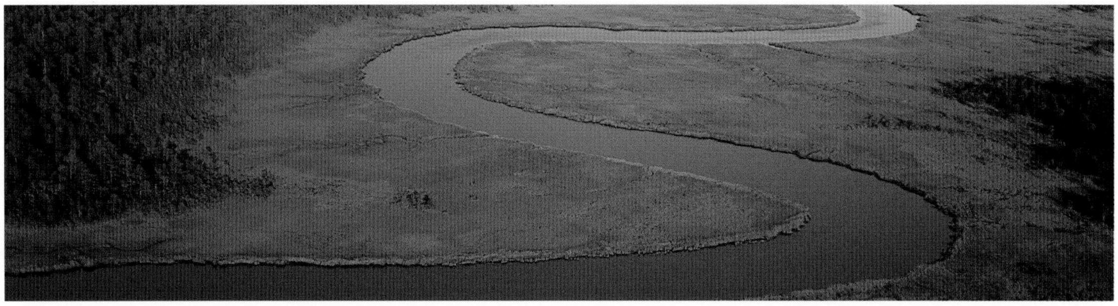

The Lowcountry of South Carolina, defined broadly as the coastal plain extending approximately 175 miles north to south (from Georgetown, SC to Savannah, GA) and roughly 50 miles inland, is an area of surpassing natural beauty punctuated by lovely coastal villages and cities such as McClellanville, Charleston, and Beaufort and barrier islands such as Bulls, Dewees, Edisto, Hunting, Fripp, Hilton Head, and Daufuskie.

The land is flat and the confluence of land and water, while a dominant geographical feature of the area, can usually only be experienced by boat or from highway bridges. The vast reaches of marshland, tidal flats and coastal forests can only be fully appreciated from an aerial perspective. From aloft, these ever-changing scenes, colored by seasonal changes of botanical hues and shifting patterns of cloud-cast shadows, present a fascinating panorama of abstract landscape vignettes.

John Trask, friend and resident of St. Helena Island near Beaufort, had the inspiration for a book which would reveal an unusual perspective of this beloved area. He convinced Jason Hawkes, English photographer and specialist in aerial imagery, to come to South Carolina and fly over the Lowcountry. Jason made several trips over a two year period, leaning precariously out of helicopters and fixed-wing aircraft to capture the dynamic patterns of sky, clouds, trees, marsh grass, sand and water. What resulted was a very unique view of one of America's most treasured, yet rapidly changing coastlines—what is, what was, and what is yet to be.

Charles L. Wyrick, Jr.

Above: Tidal creek. Daufuskie Island.

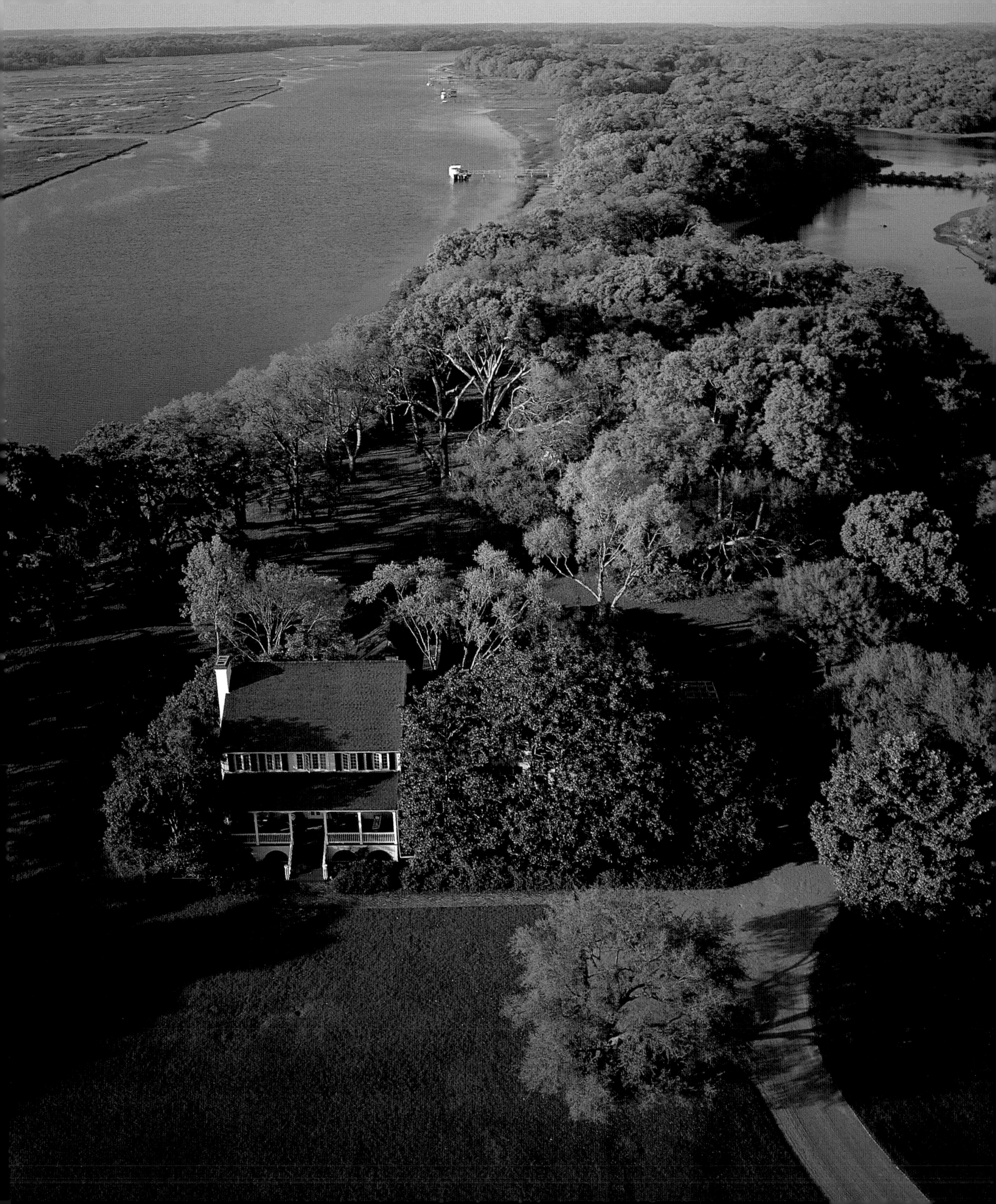

INTRODUCTION

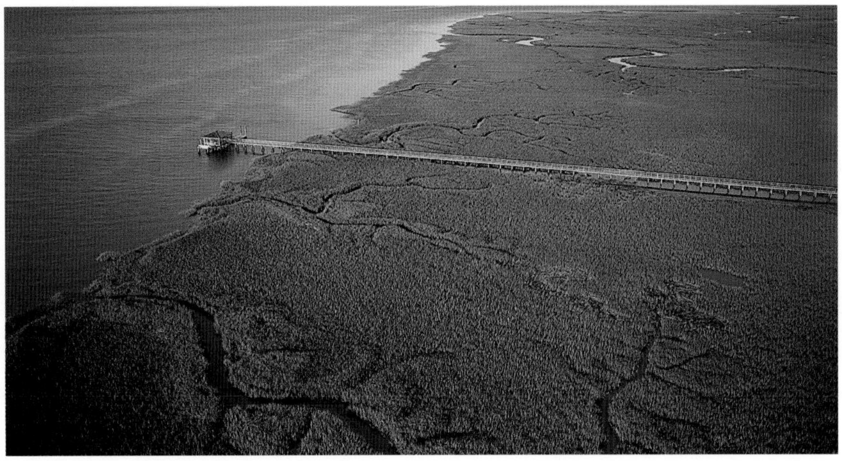

For most of us who live in the South Carolina Lowcountry, our physical perspective with the land has been limited by our everyday experiences as viewed from our own physical height or, at most, as seen from an upstairs window.

I recall the first time that I experienced a new perspective of this otherwise flat land that we call the Lowcountry. It was from the fourth floor of a grand Bay Street house. Looking down, through the arched branches of live oak trees onto the streetscape below, I made a new discovery. It was that there was another world right around me, but one that I had not been a part of before. It was the world of elevation, of physical height.

It is my hope that as we look at these photographic images of the Lowcountry from the air, they will bring a new perspective to our lives – not just physically, but also philosophically. Indeed, perhaps they will give us a more personal understanding of T. S. Eliot's words:

We shall not cease from exploring.
And the end of all our exploring
Will be to arrive where we started
And know the place for the first time.

To my family, my friends, and to all who love this land, I say let us keep exploring until that time comes when we shall pass into some far distant experience across the waters, marshes, woods, and fields of the South Carolina Lowcountry.

John M. Trask, Jr.

Left: Orange Grove, St. Helena Island.

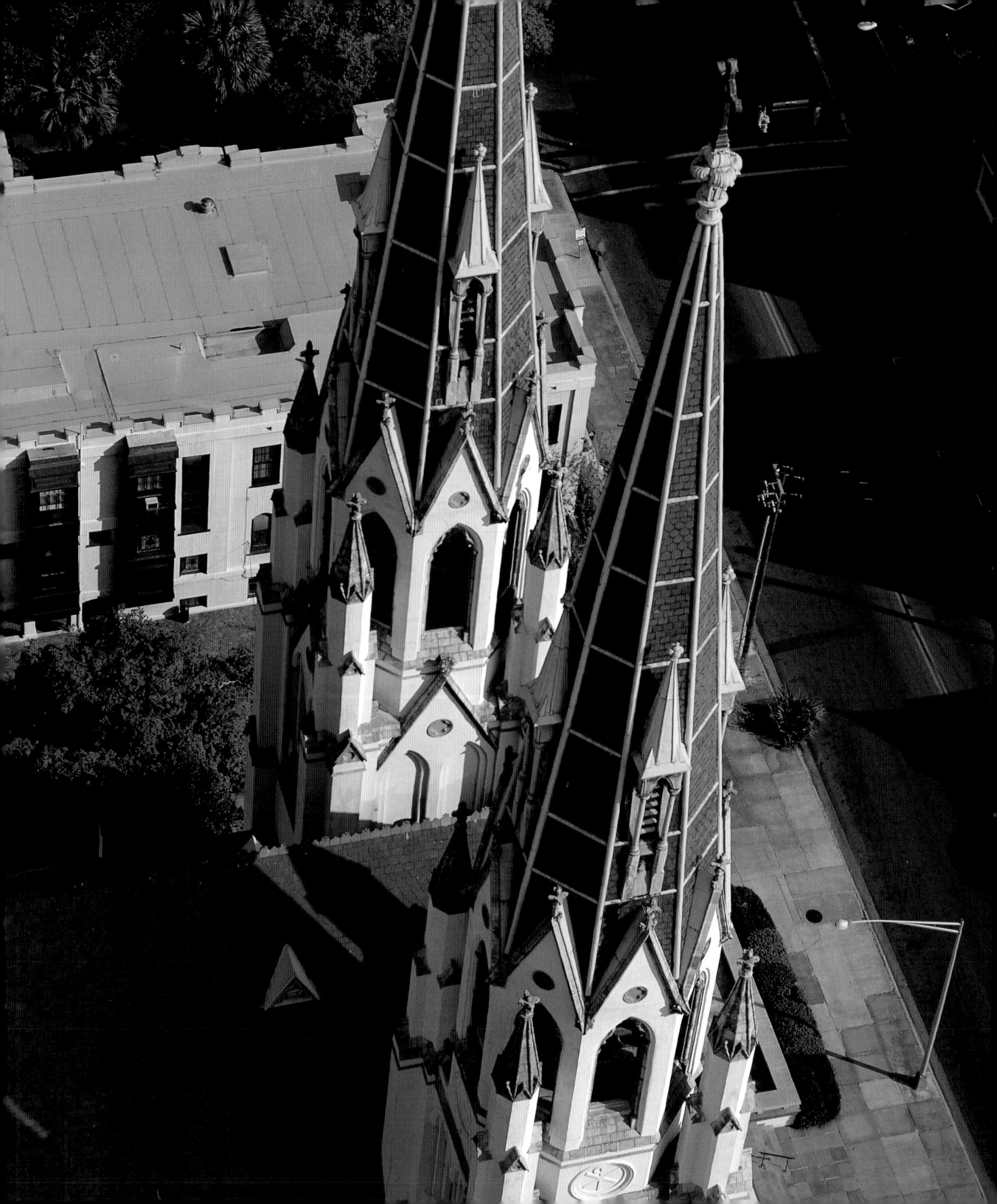

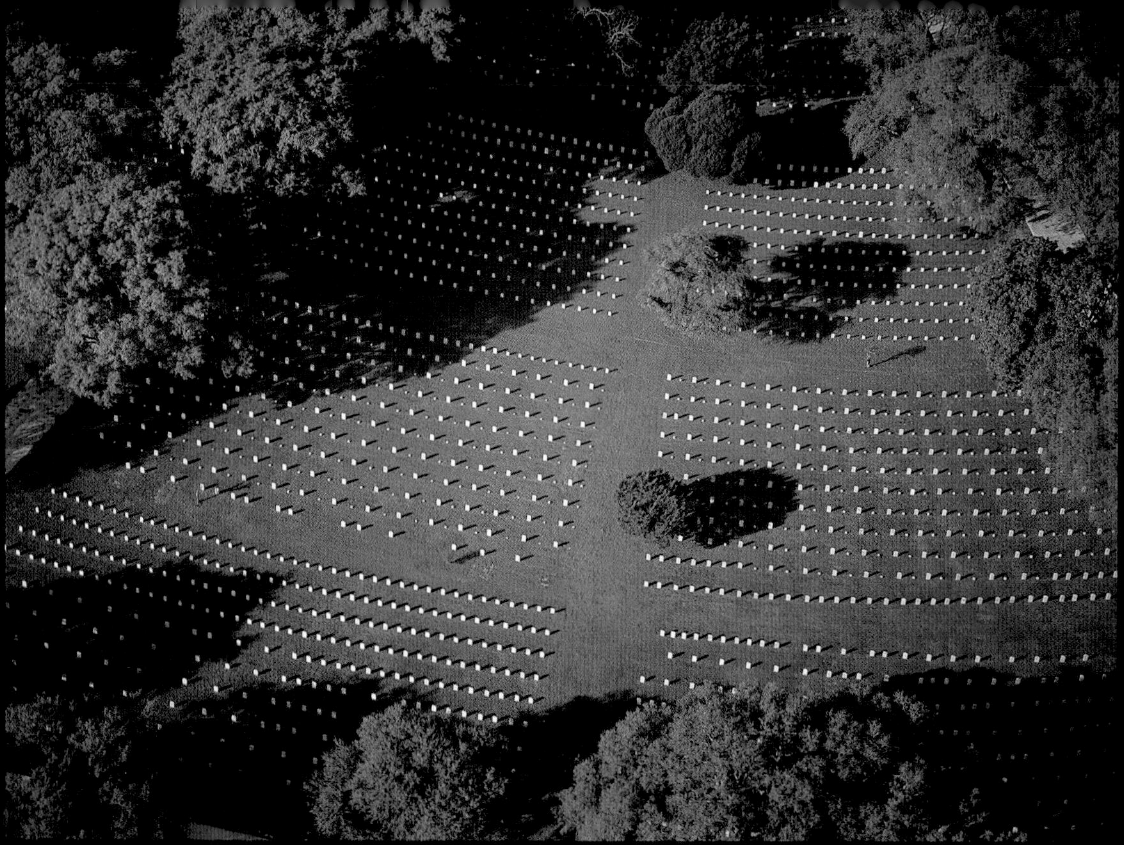

Above: Beaufort National Cemetery.

Left: Cathedral of St. John the Baptist, Savannah

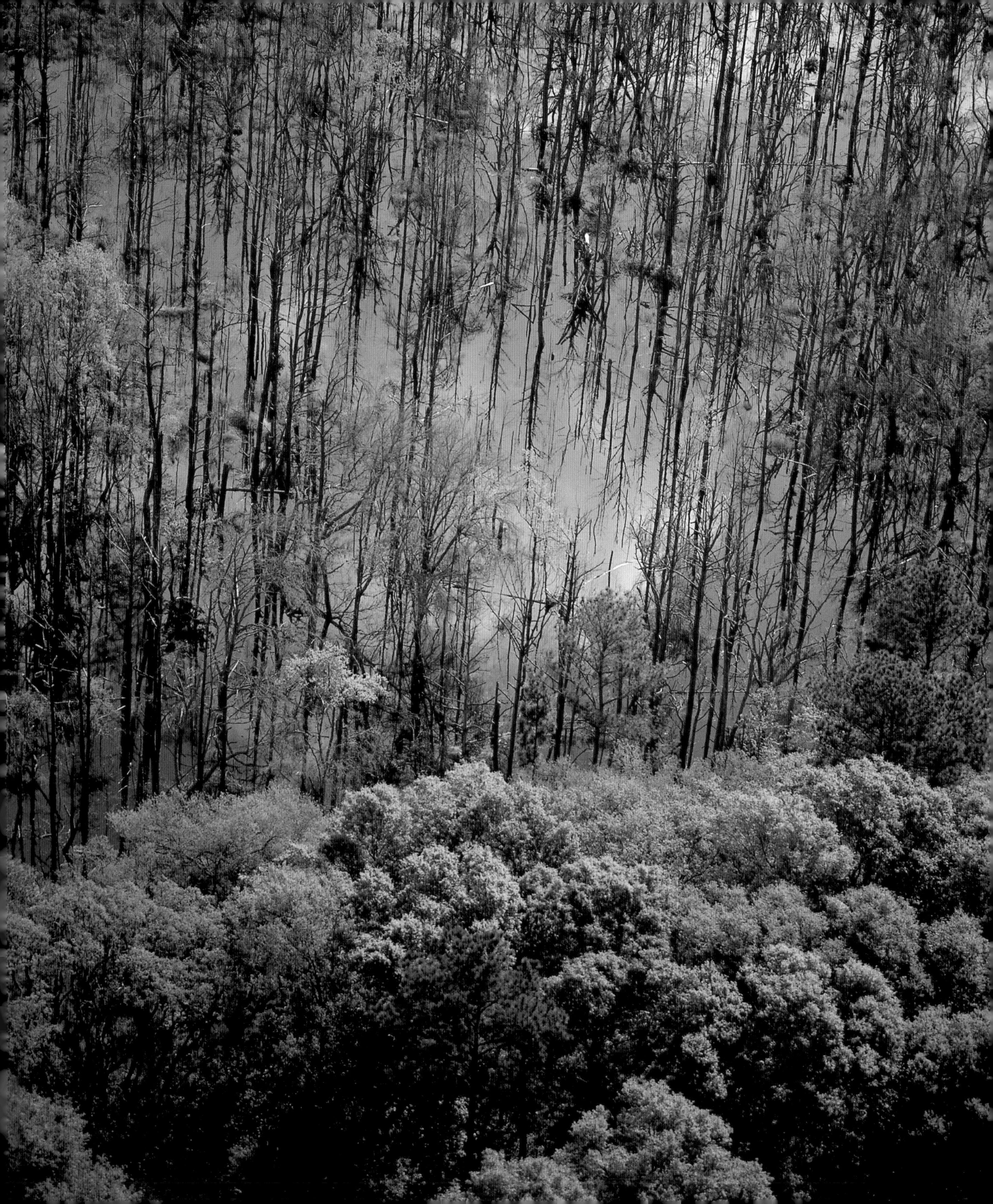

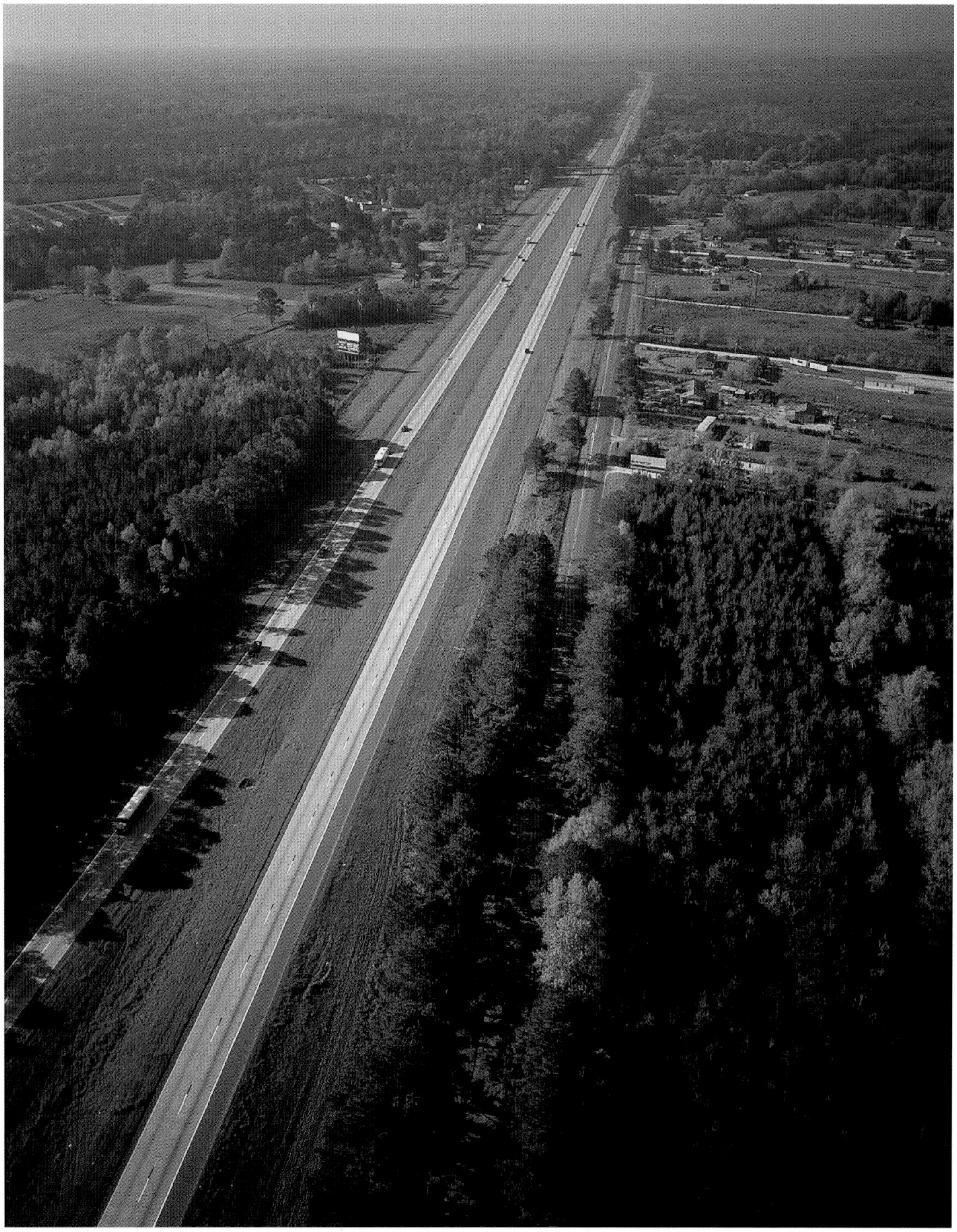

Above: Highway 17.

Left: Flooded former rice fields. Beaufort County.

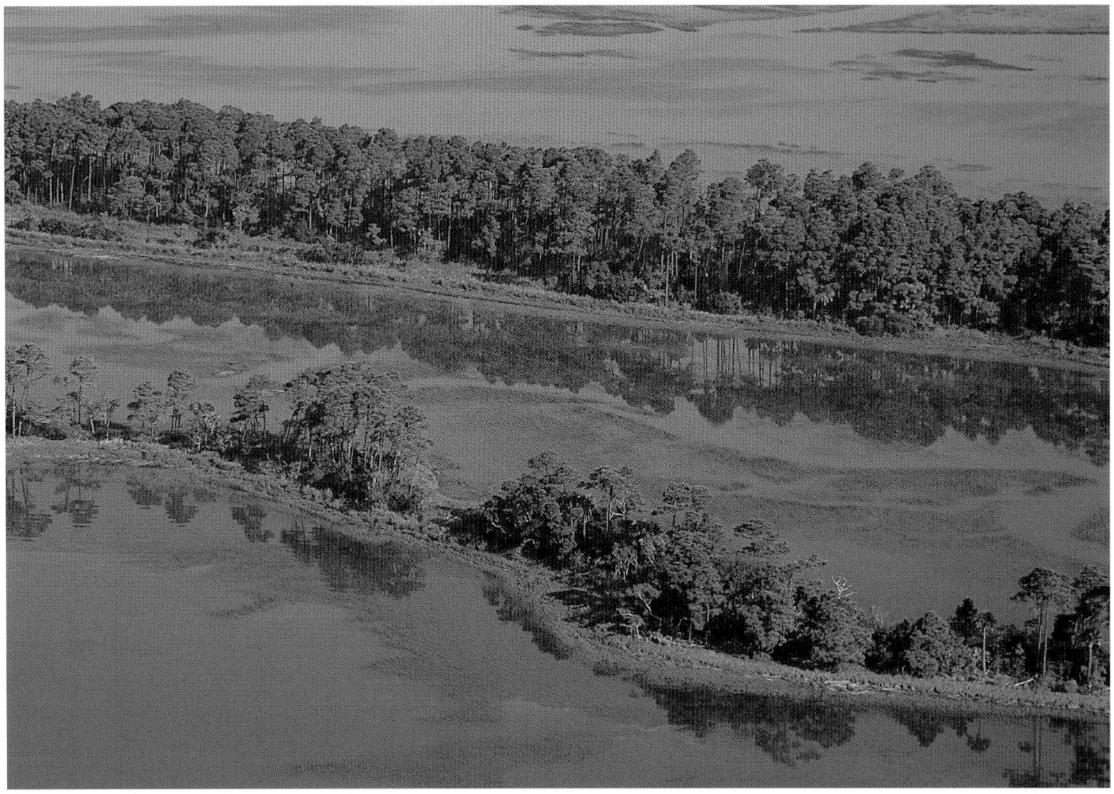

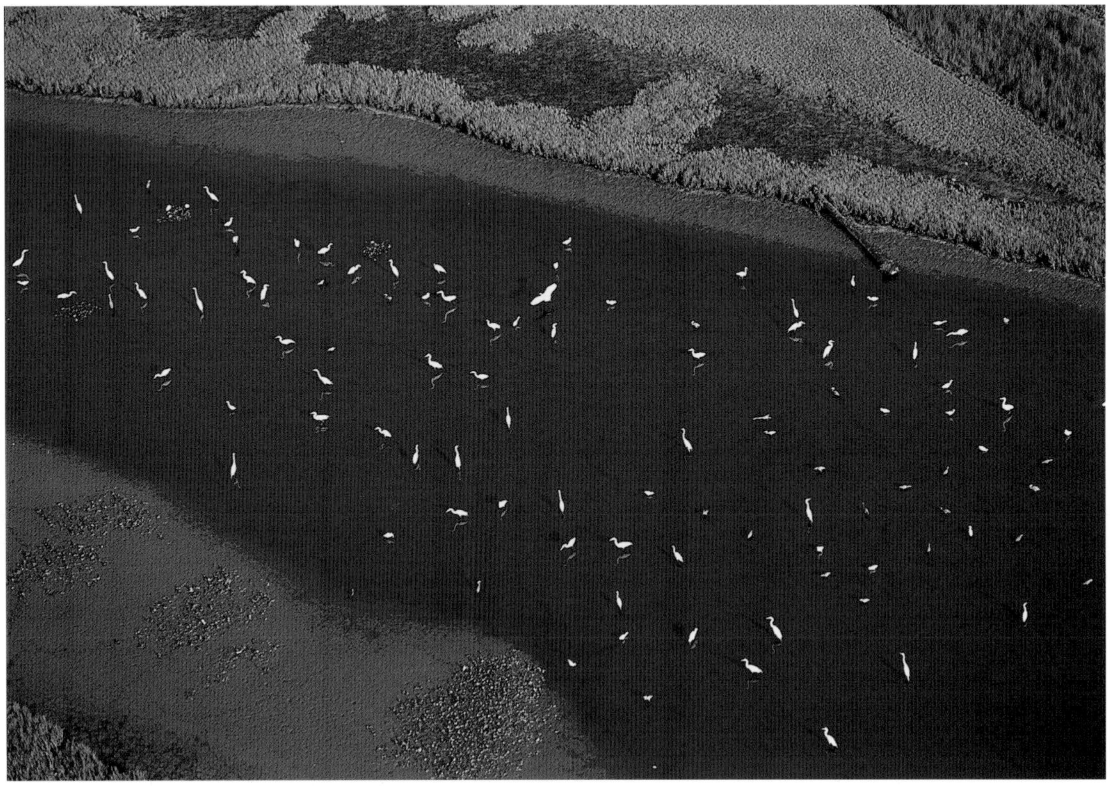

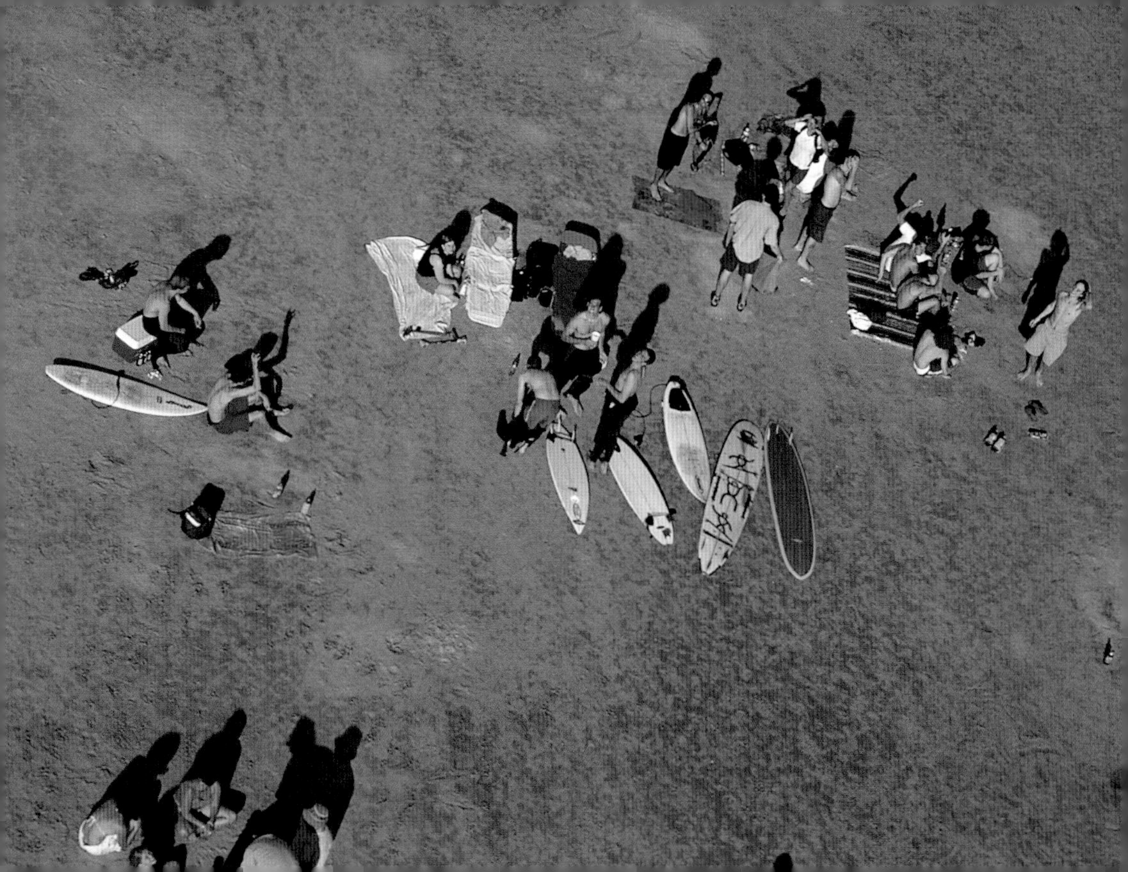

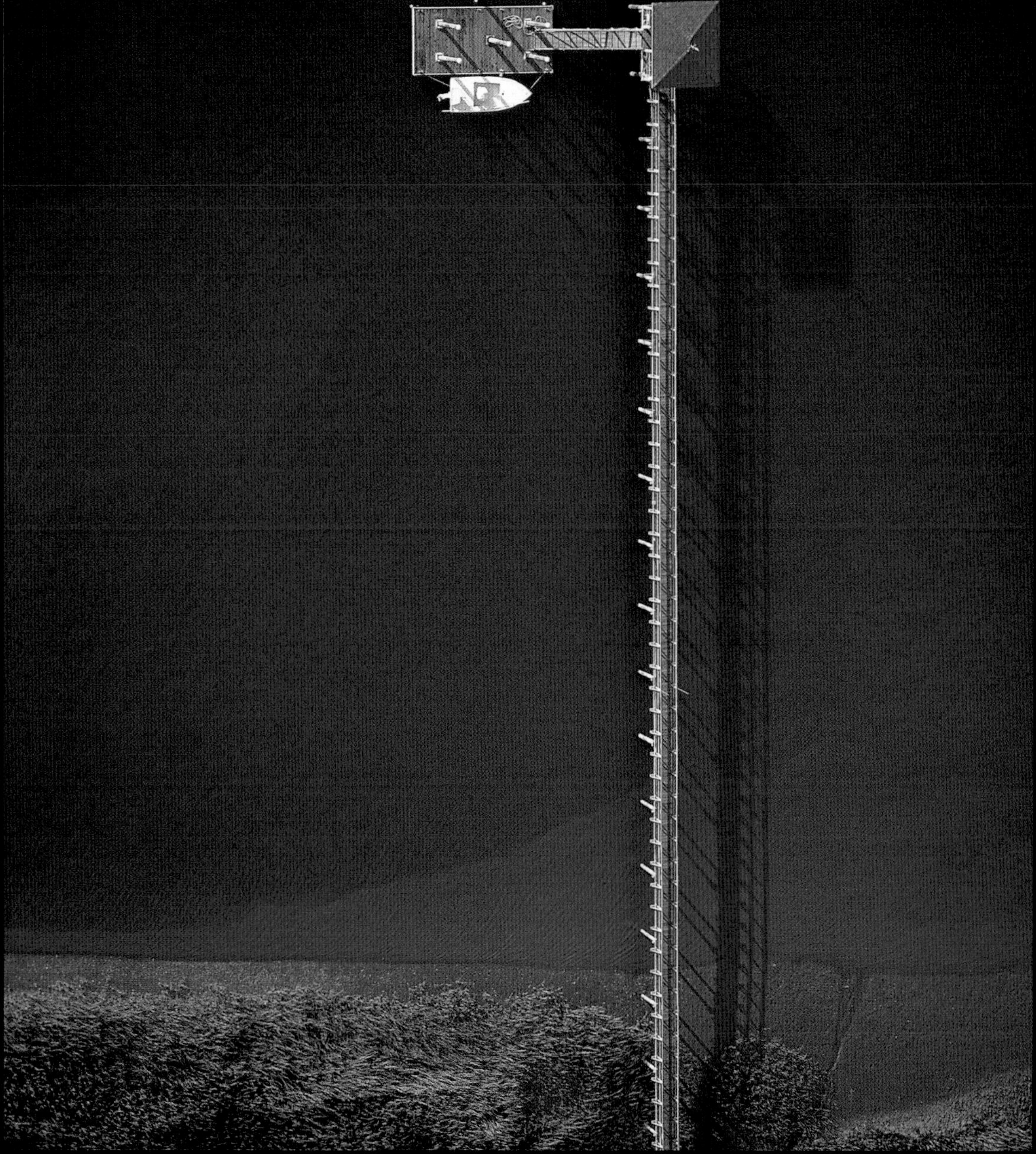

Above: Boat dock. Beaufort River.

Left: Tomato fields at Orange Grove. St. Helena Island.

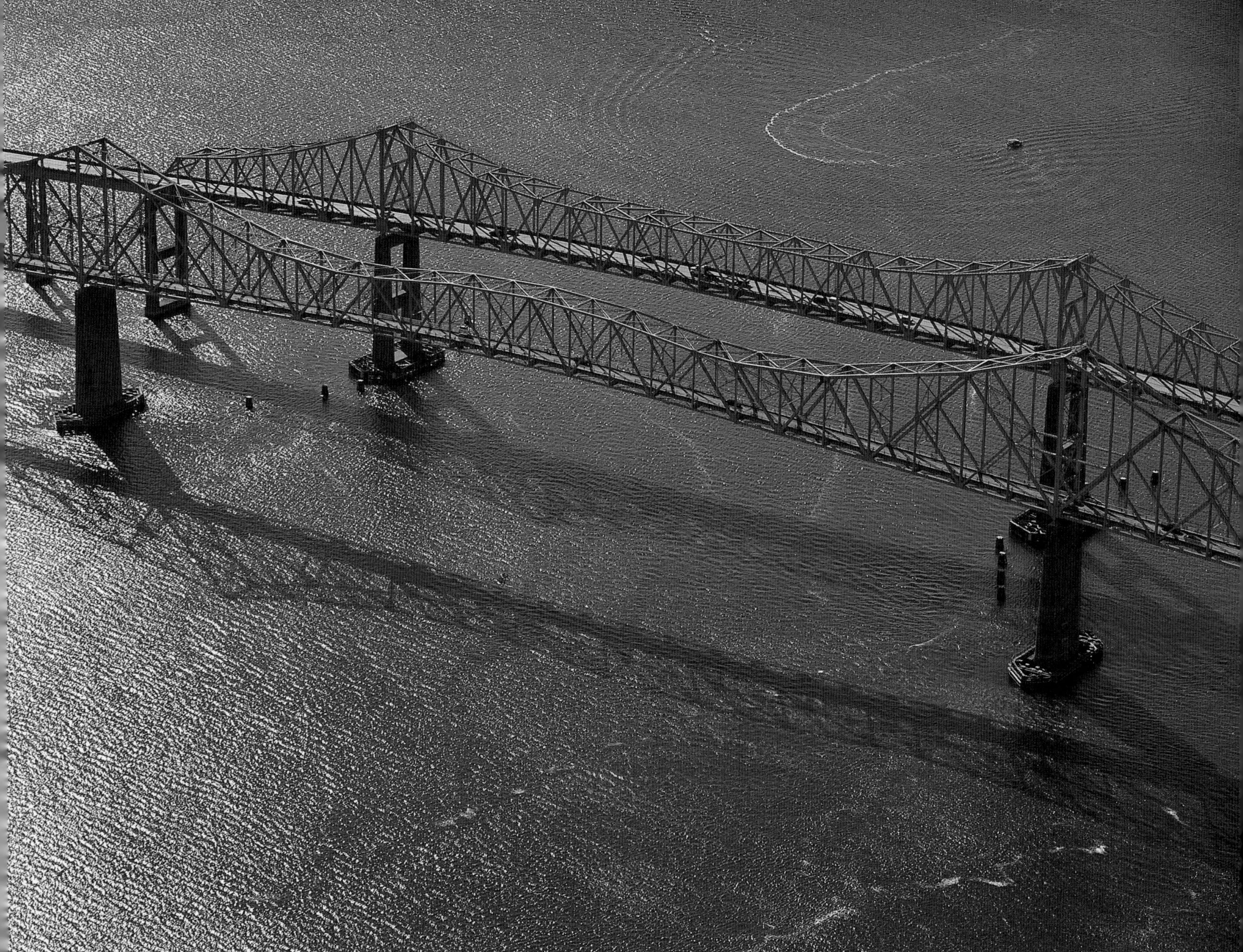

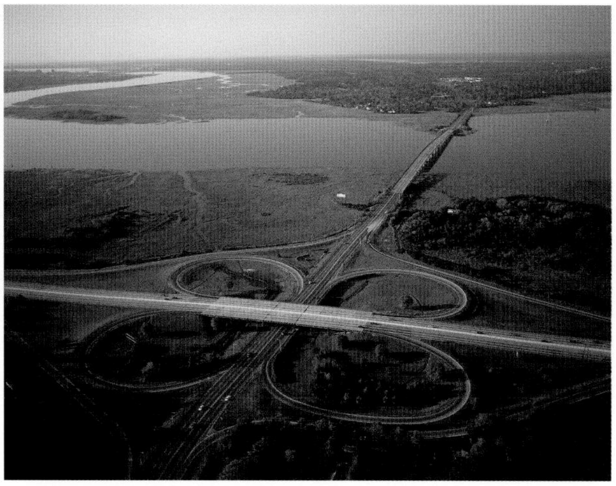

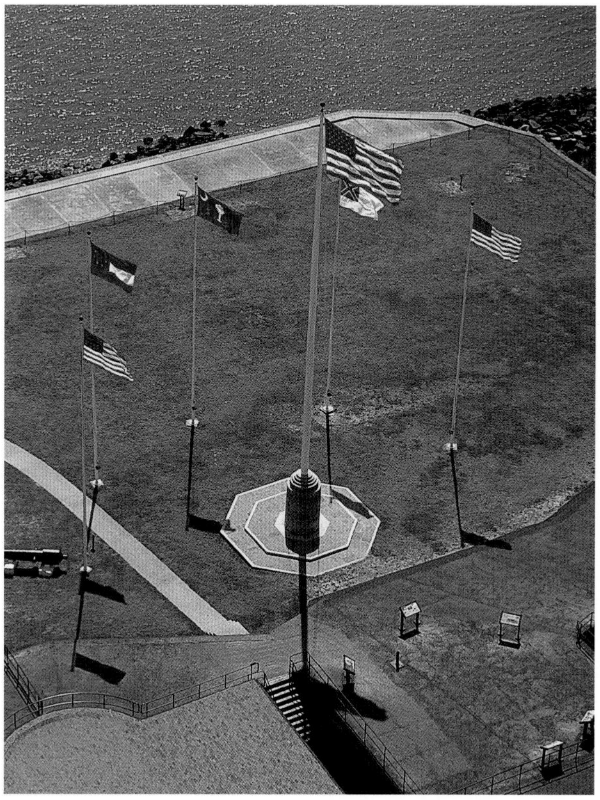

Top: Interstate 26 and memorial bridge. Charleston.

Bottom: Flags flying at Fort Sumter.

Left: Cooper River Bridges. Charleston.

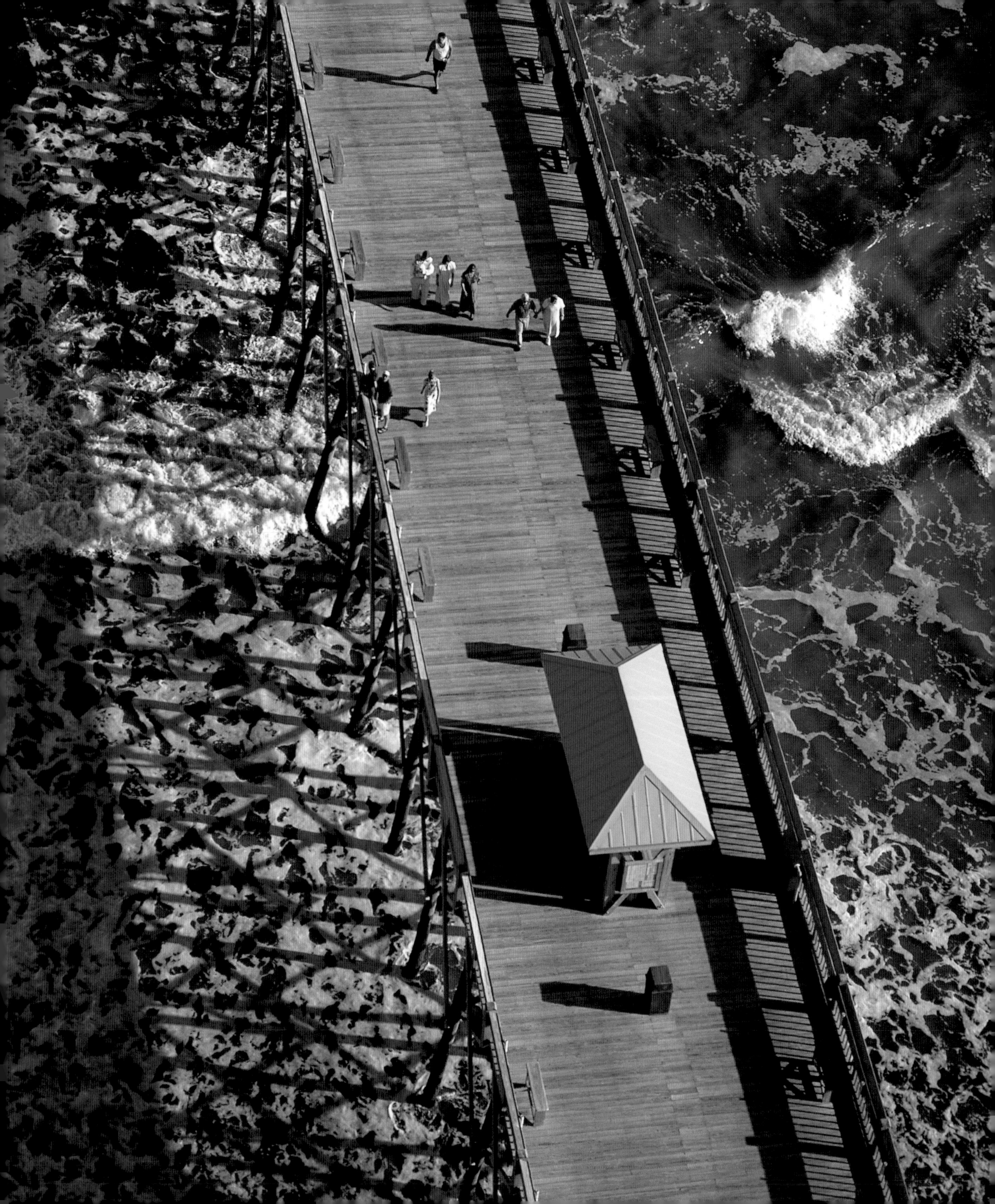

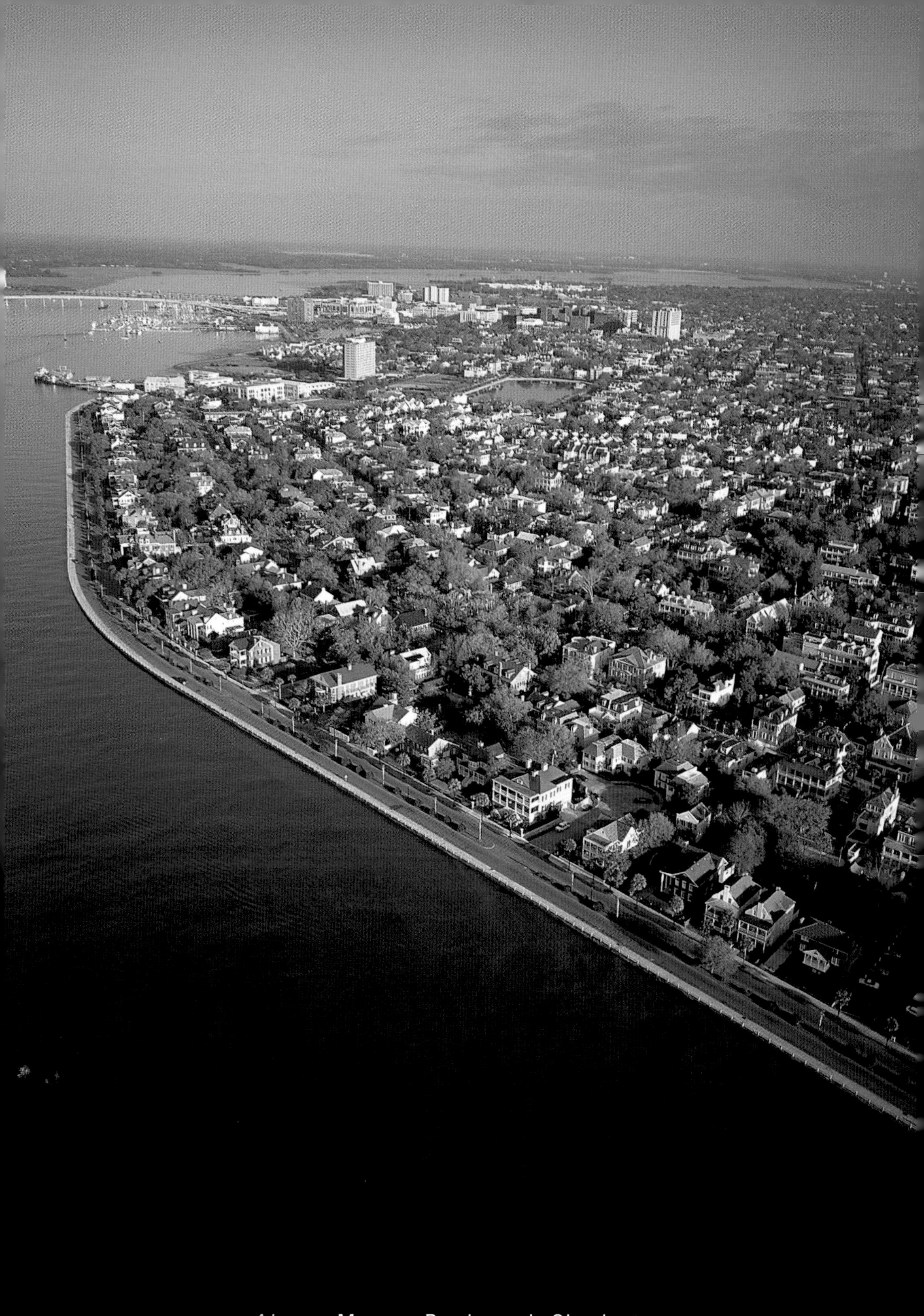

Above: Murray Boulevard, Charleston

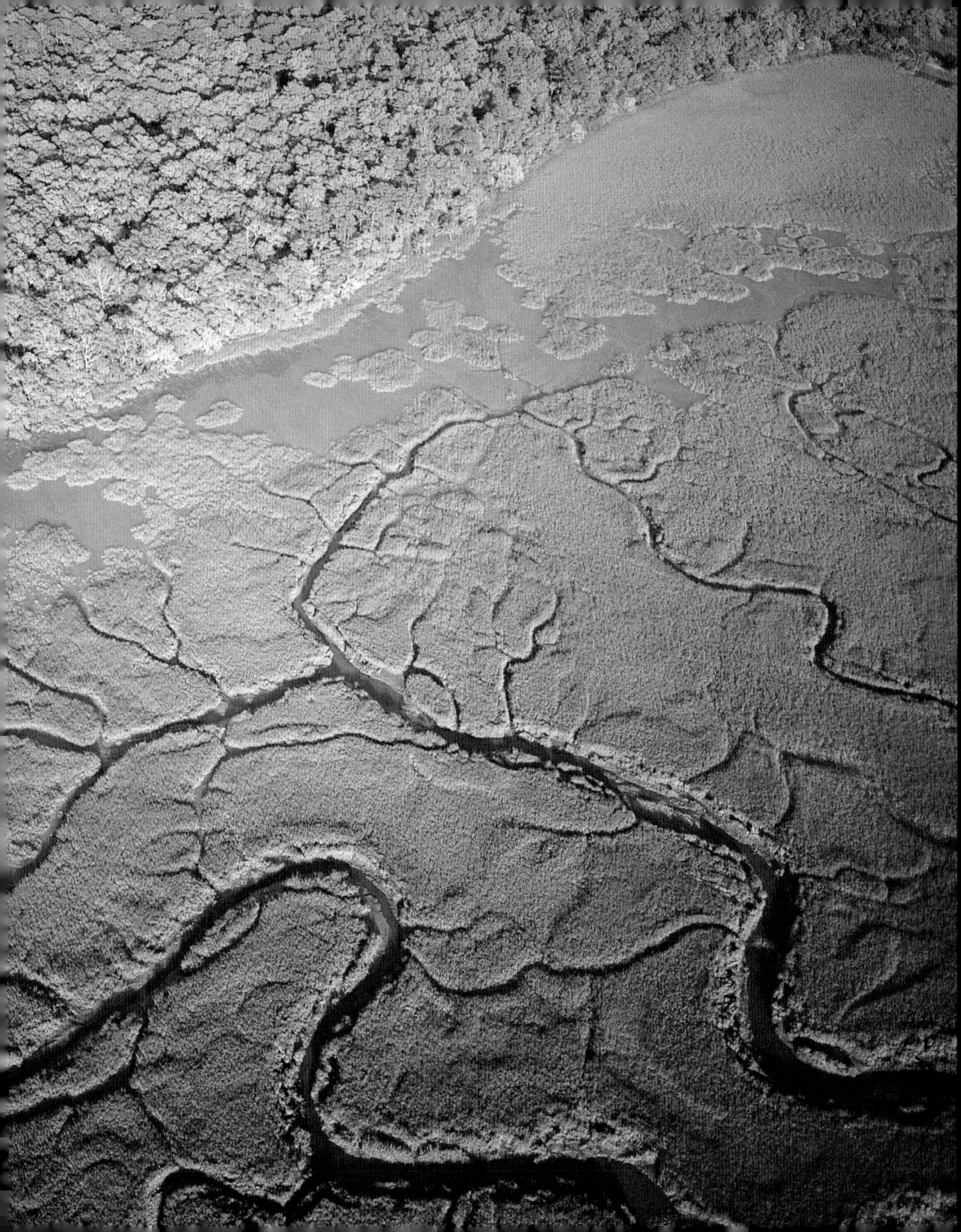

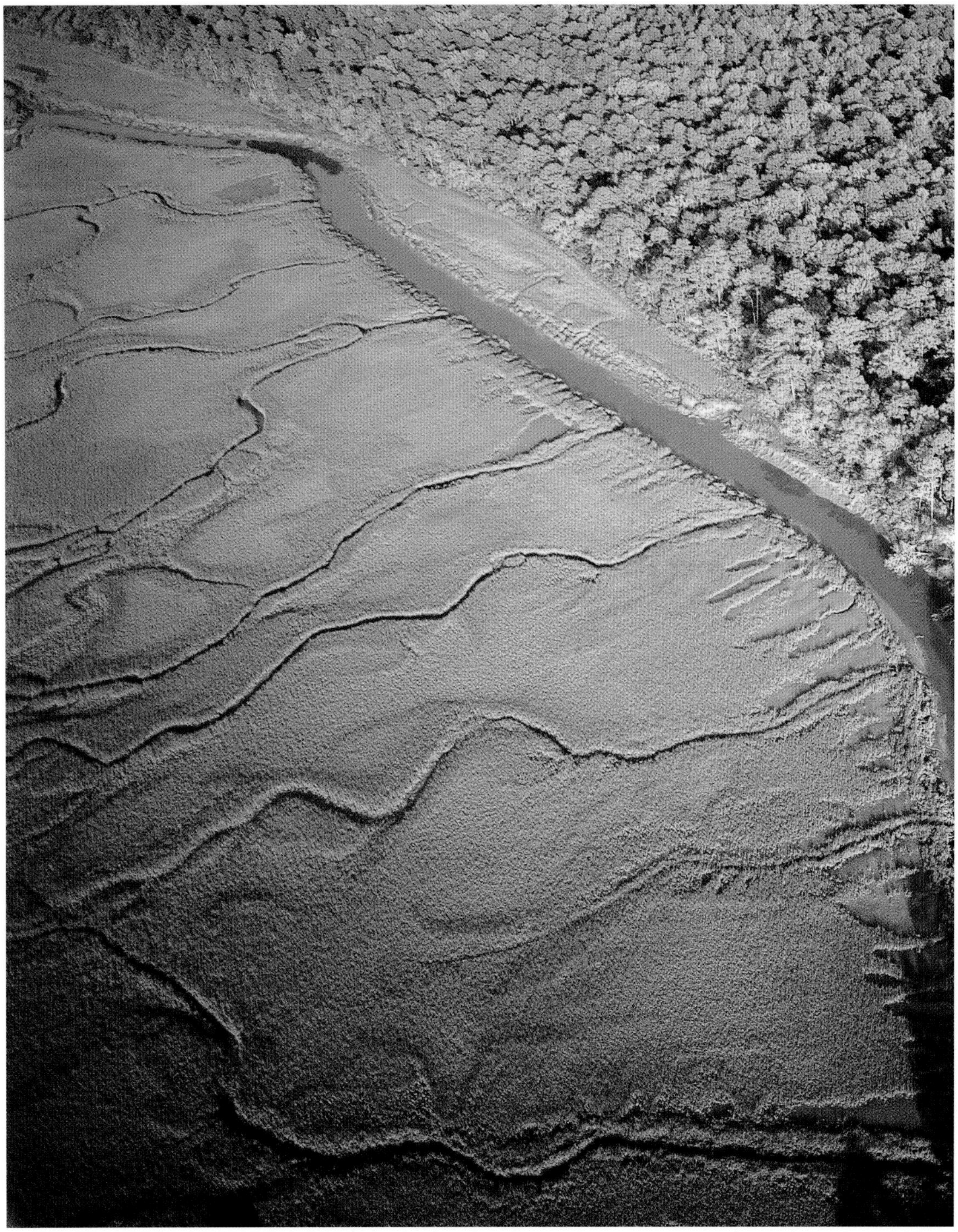

Left and Above: Tidal marsh creeks. St. Helena Island.

Next Page: Shrimp boat. Beaufort River.

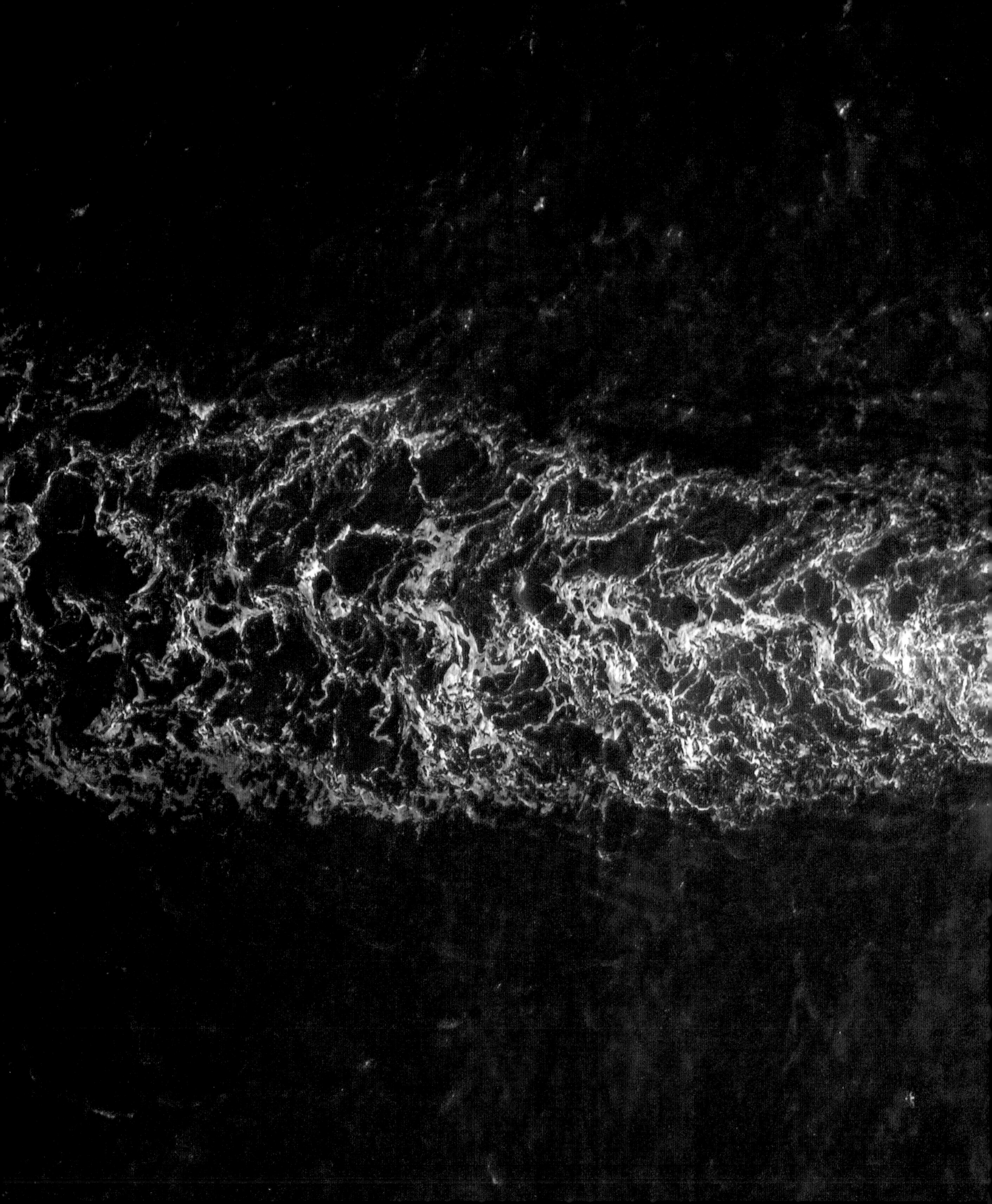

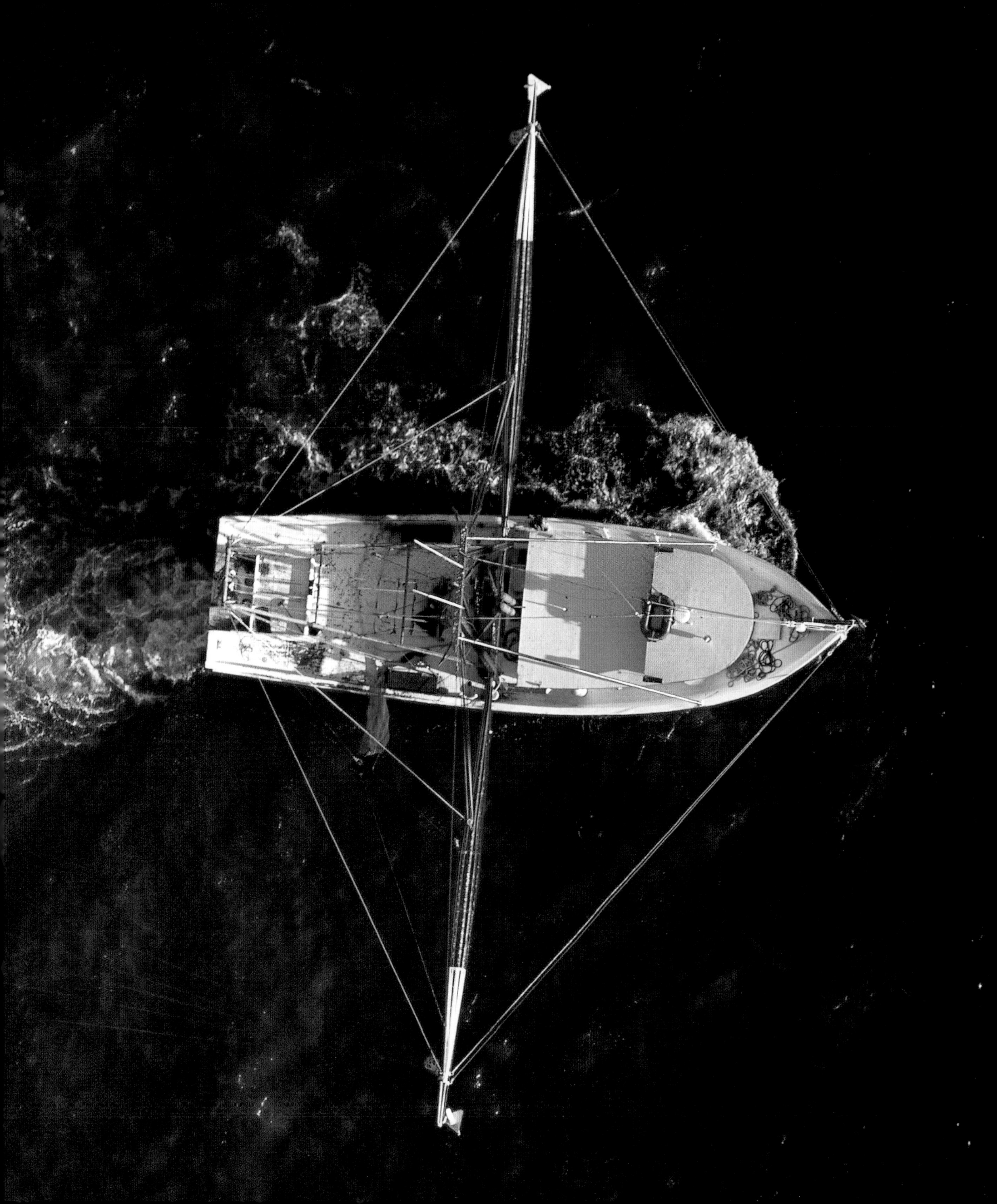

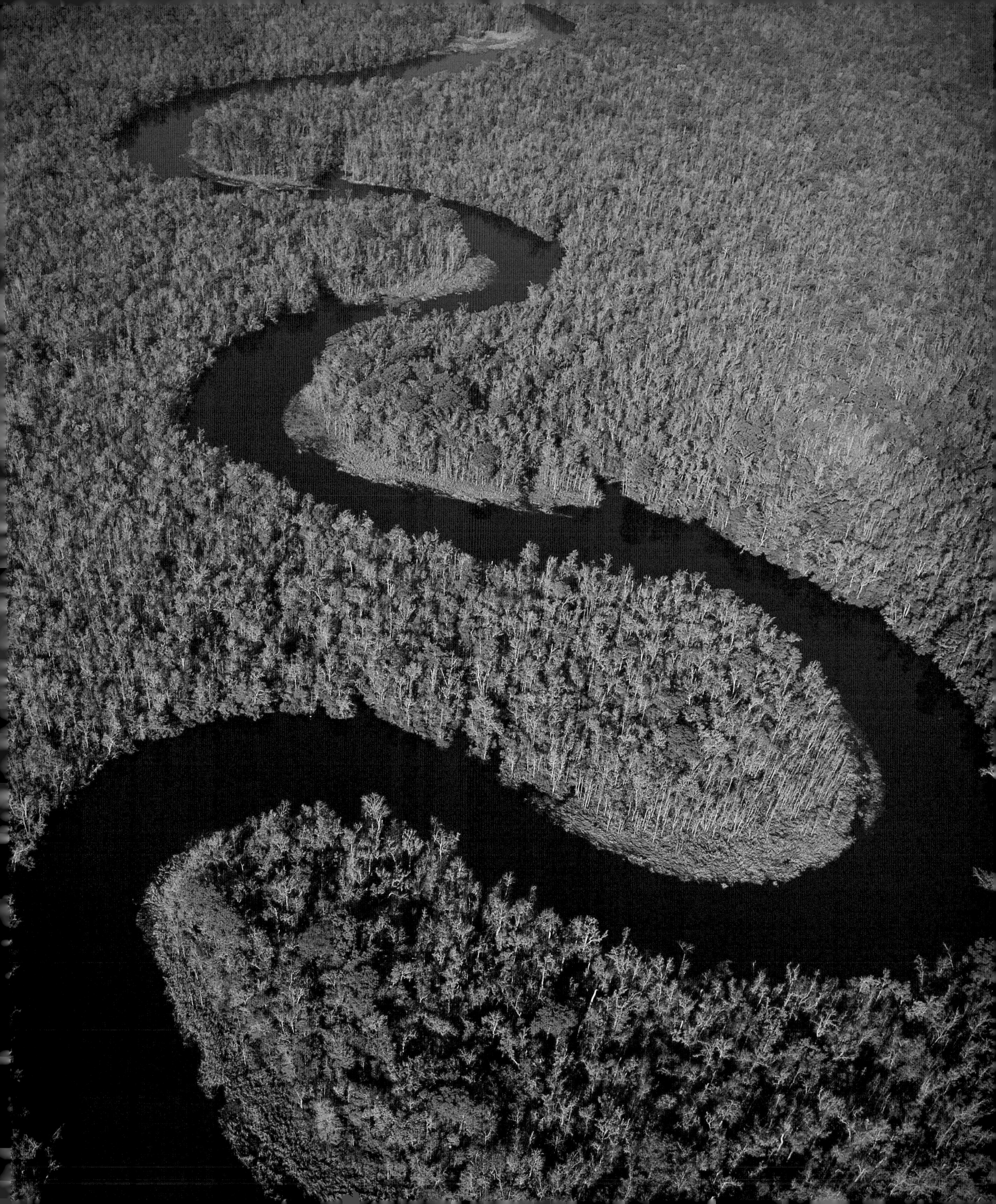

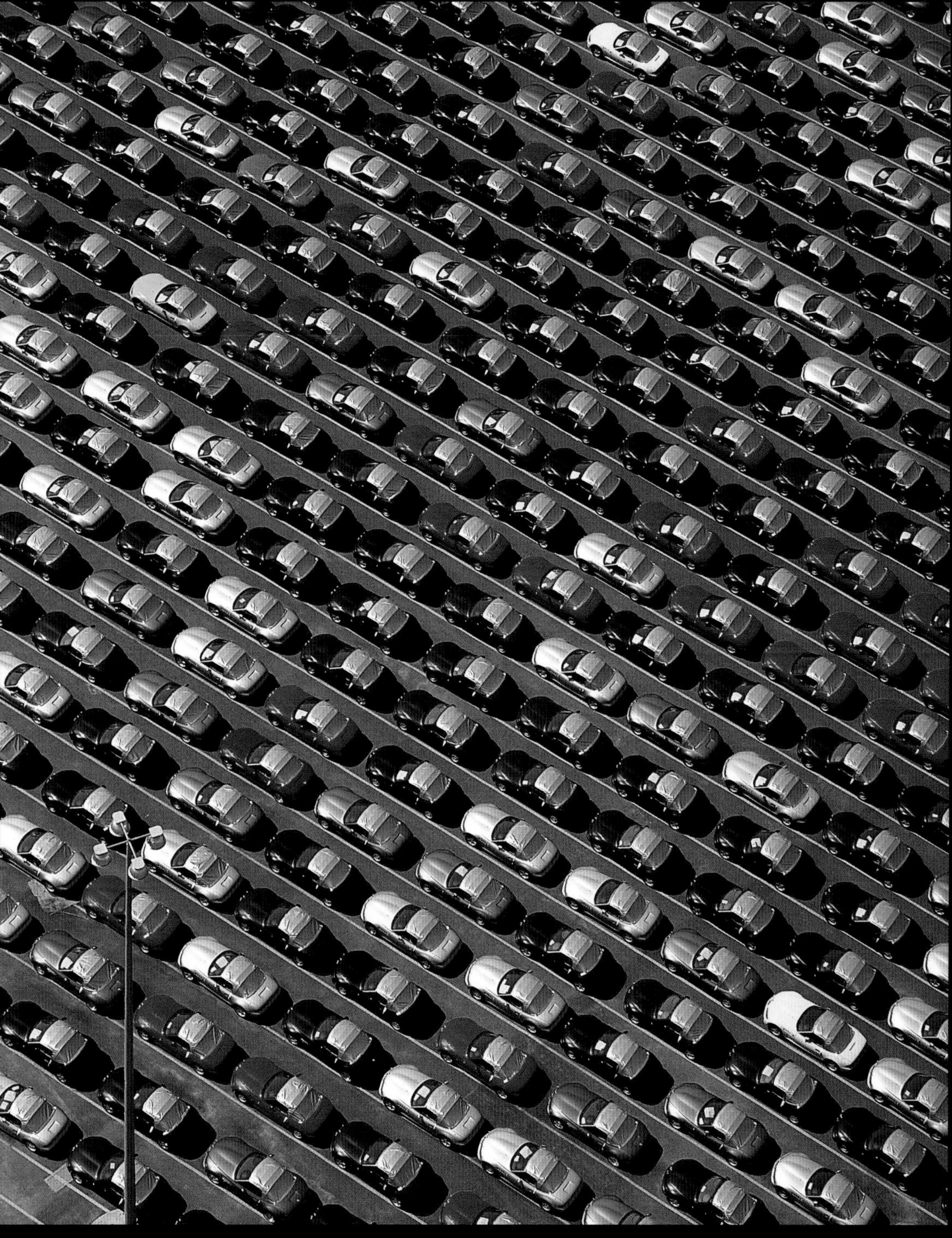

Above: BMW Z3s awaiting shipment. Port of Charleston.

Left: Combahee River.

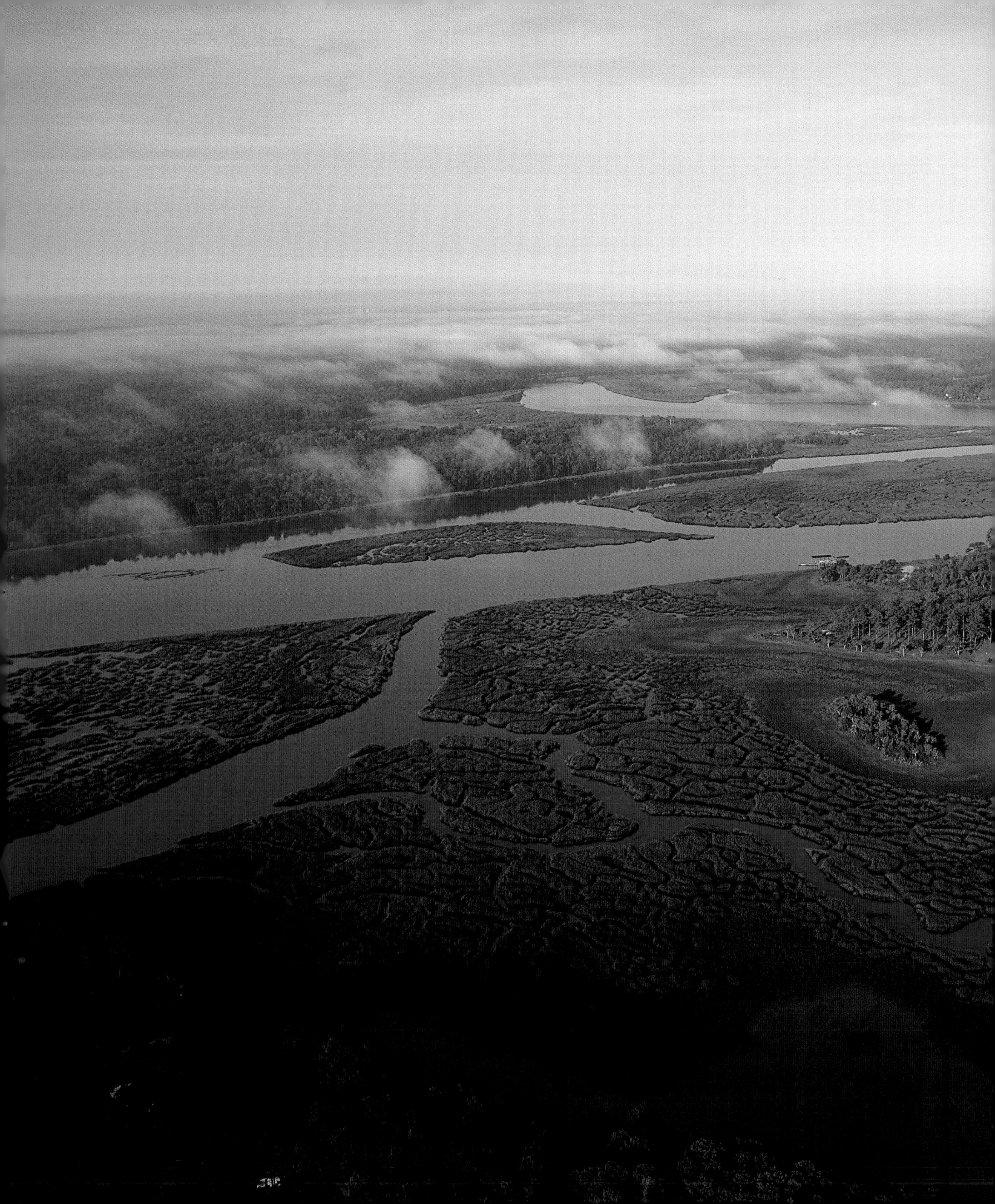

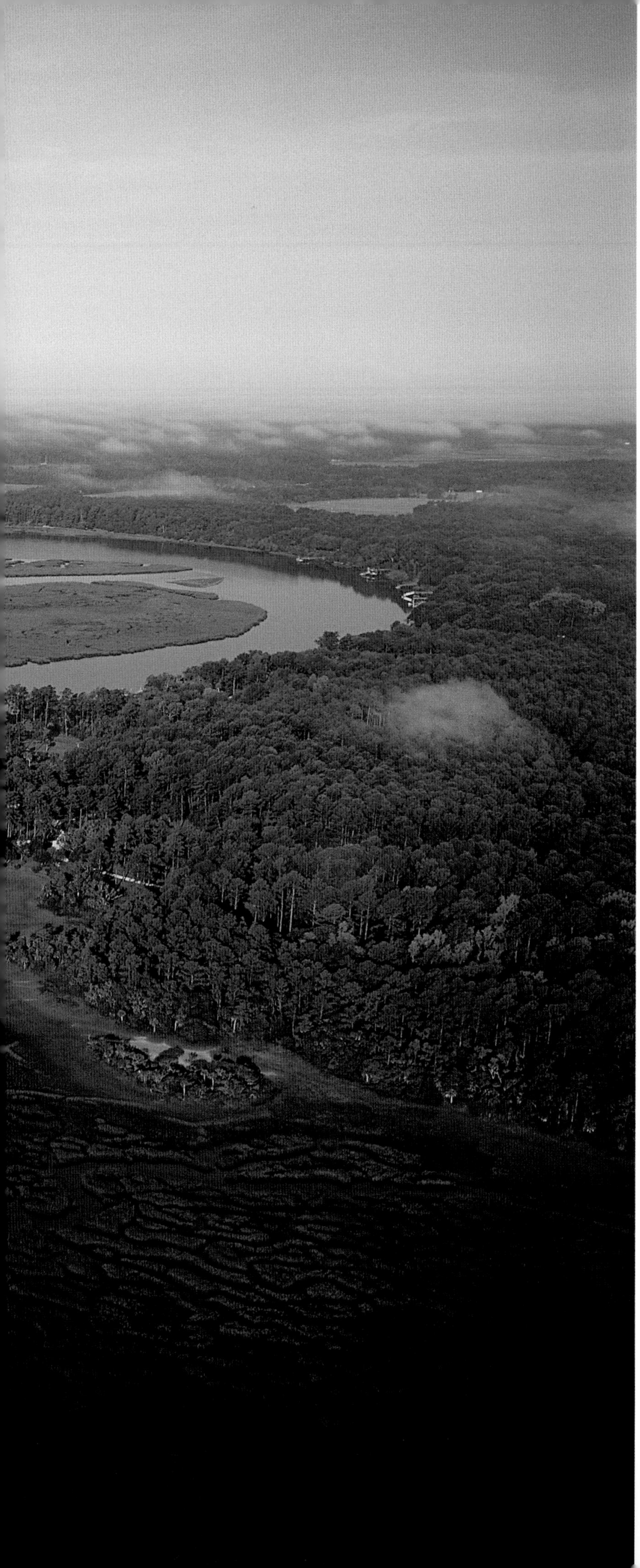

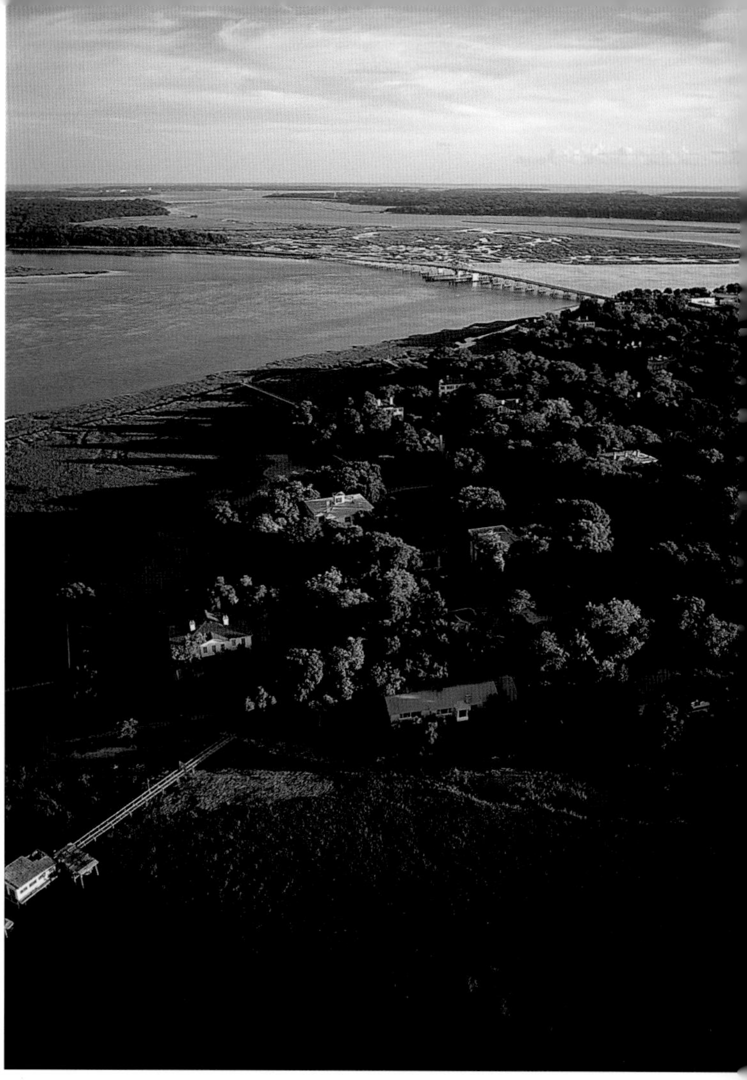

Above: Beaufort.

Left: May River, near Bluffton.

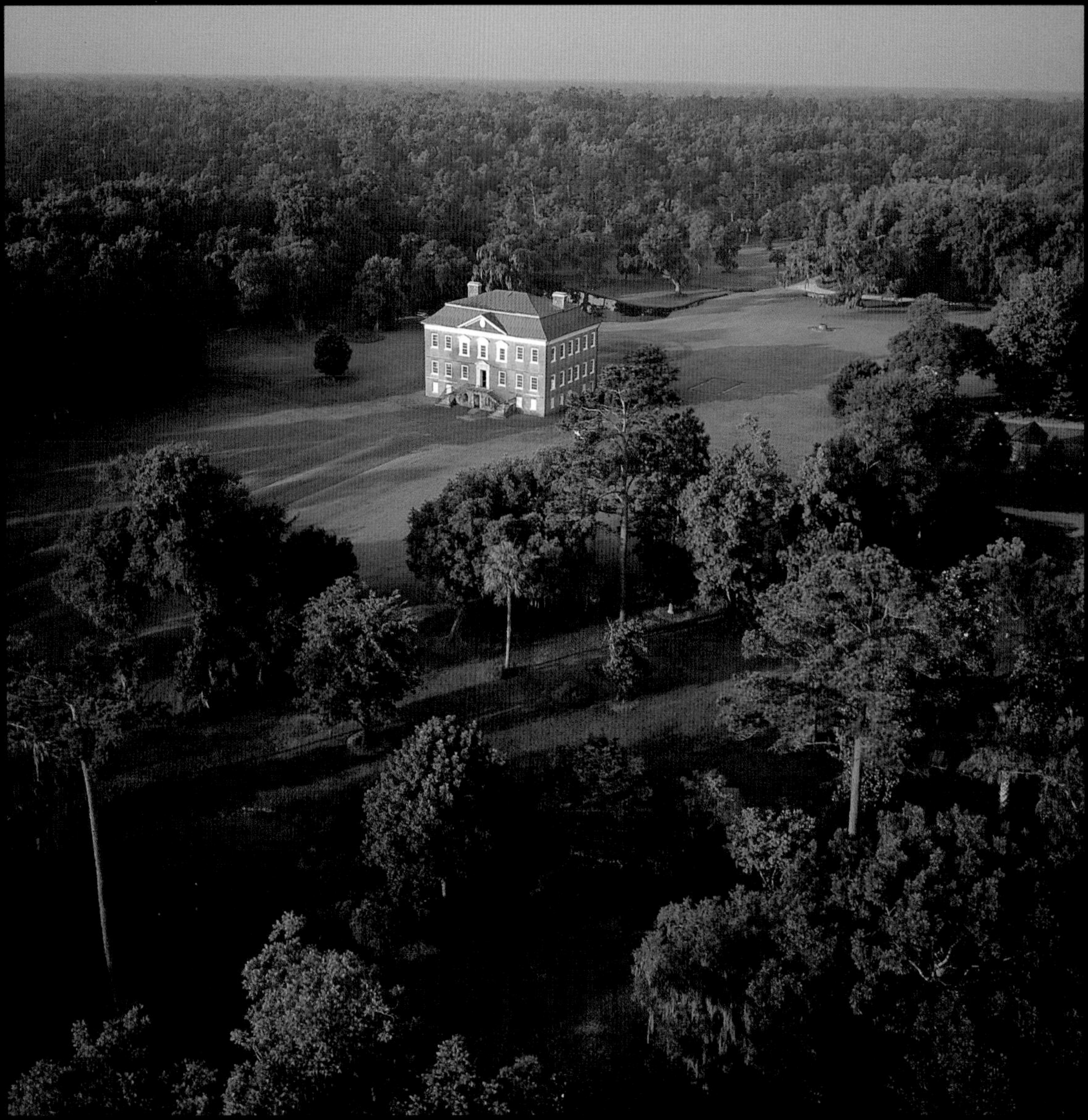

Above: Drayton Hall. Charleston.

Right: Low tide near Stono Inlet.

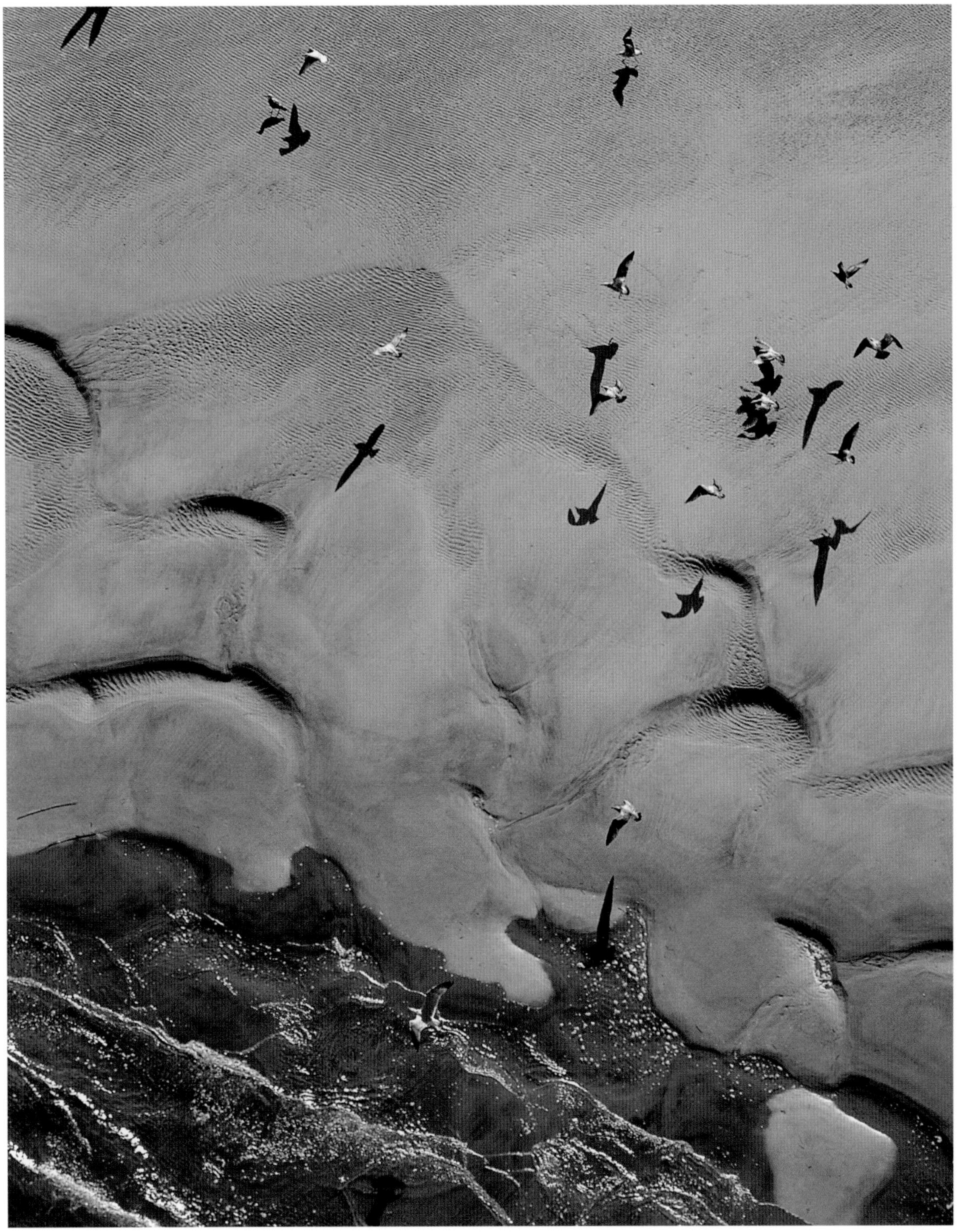

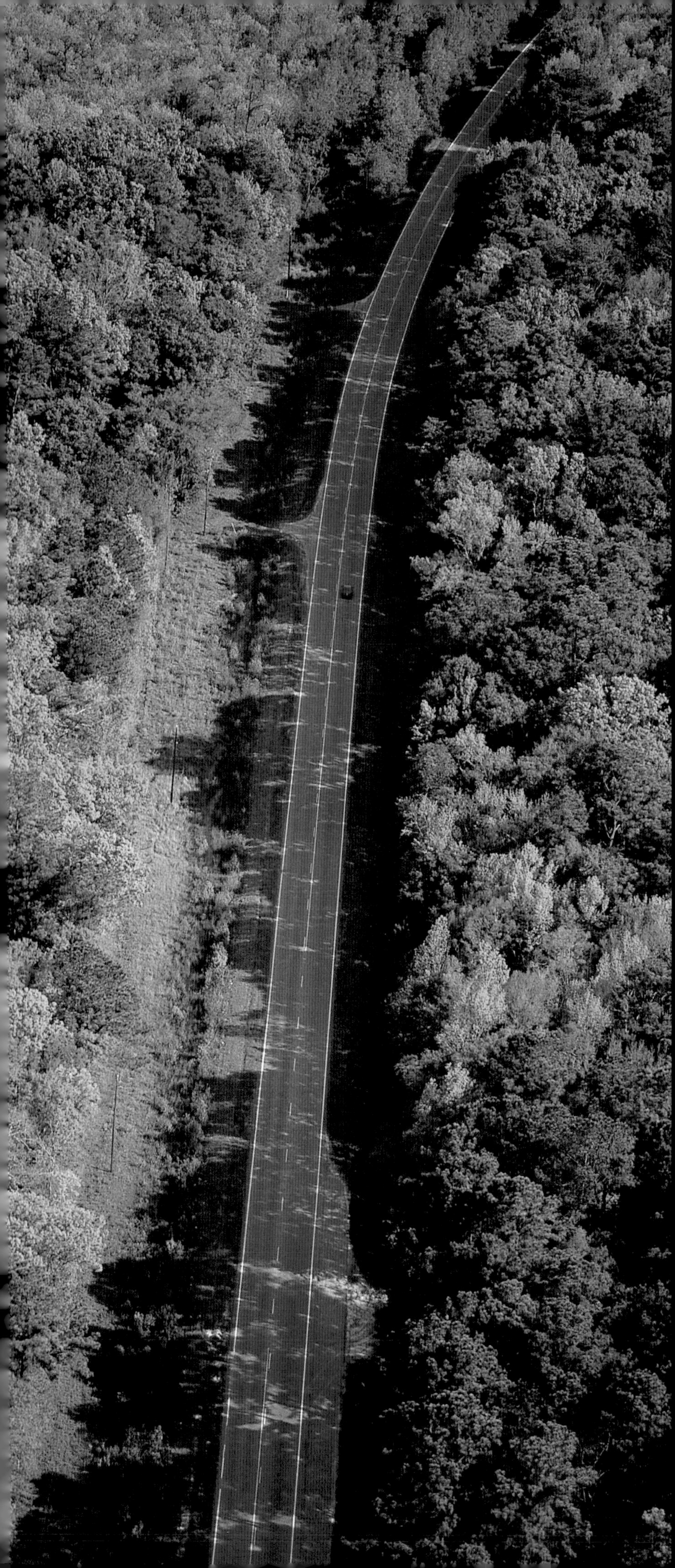

Right: Boat docks. Johns Island.

Left: Highway 17. ACE Basin.

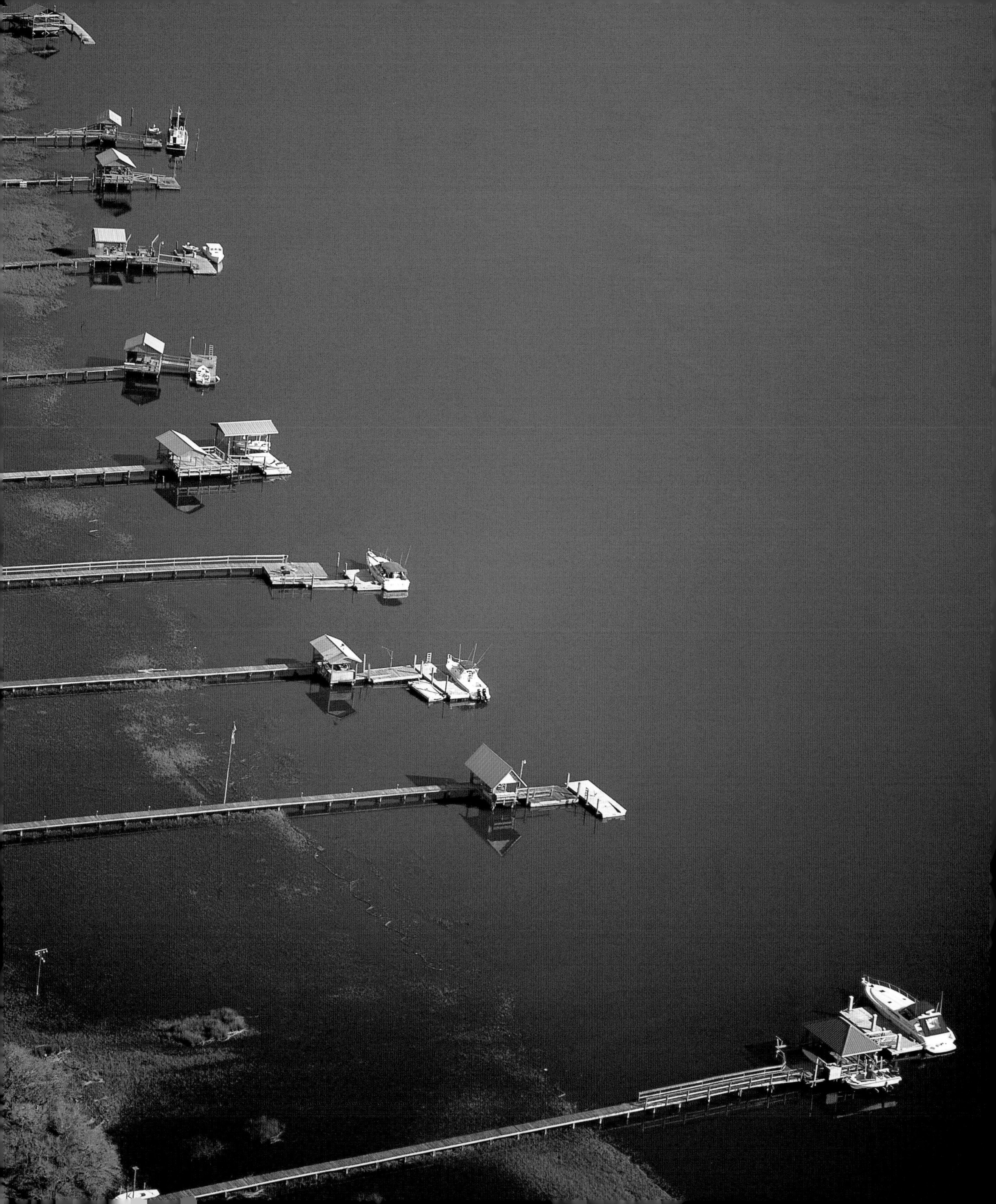

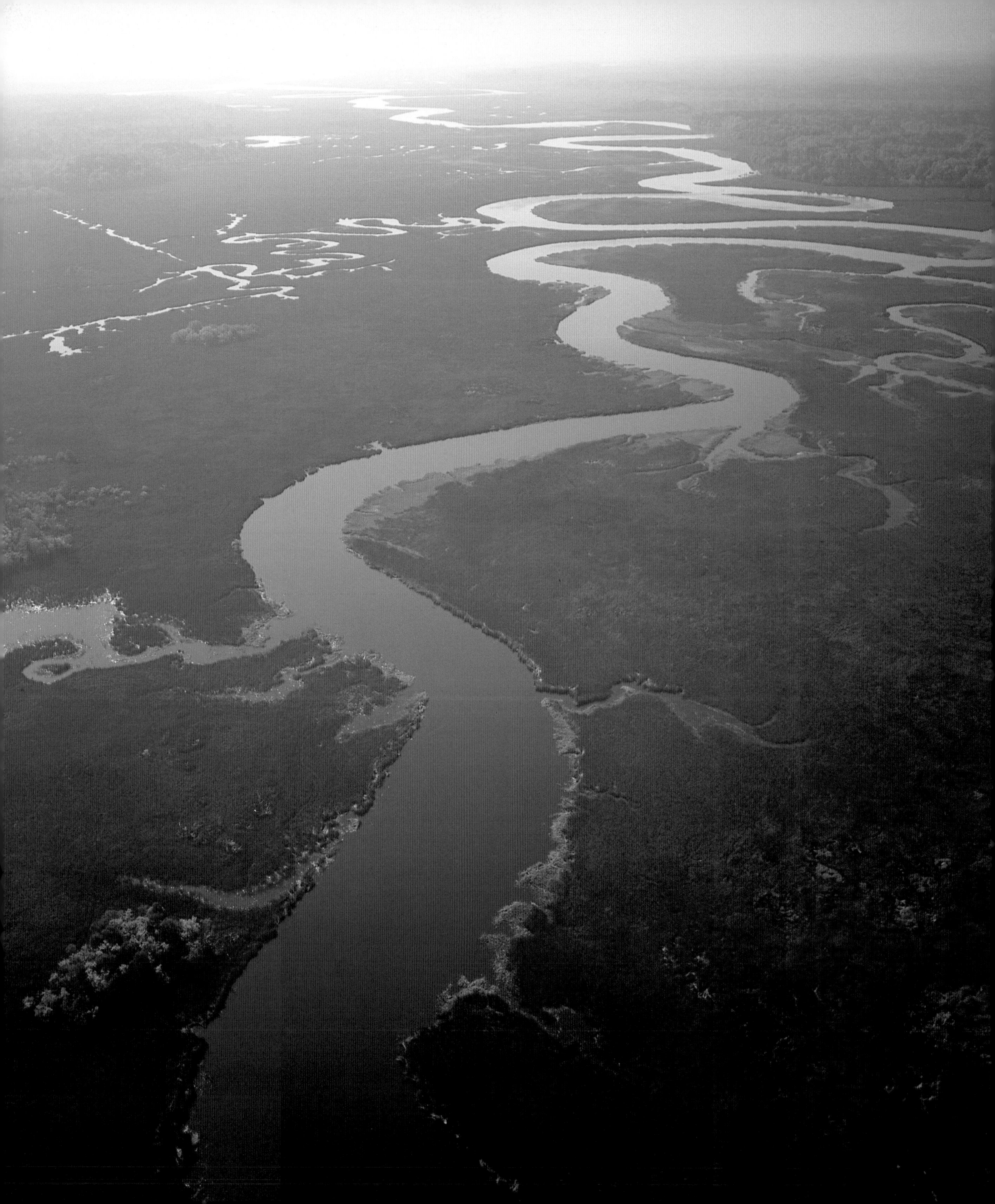

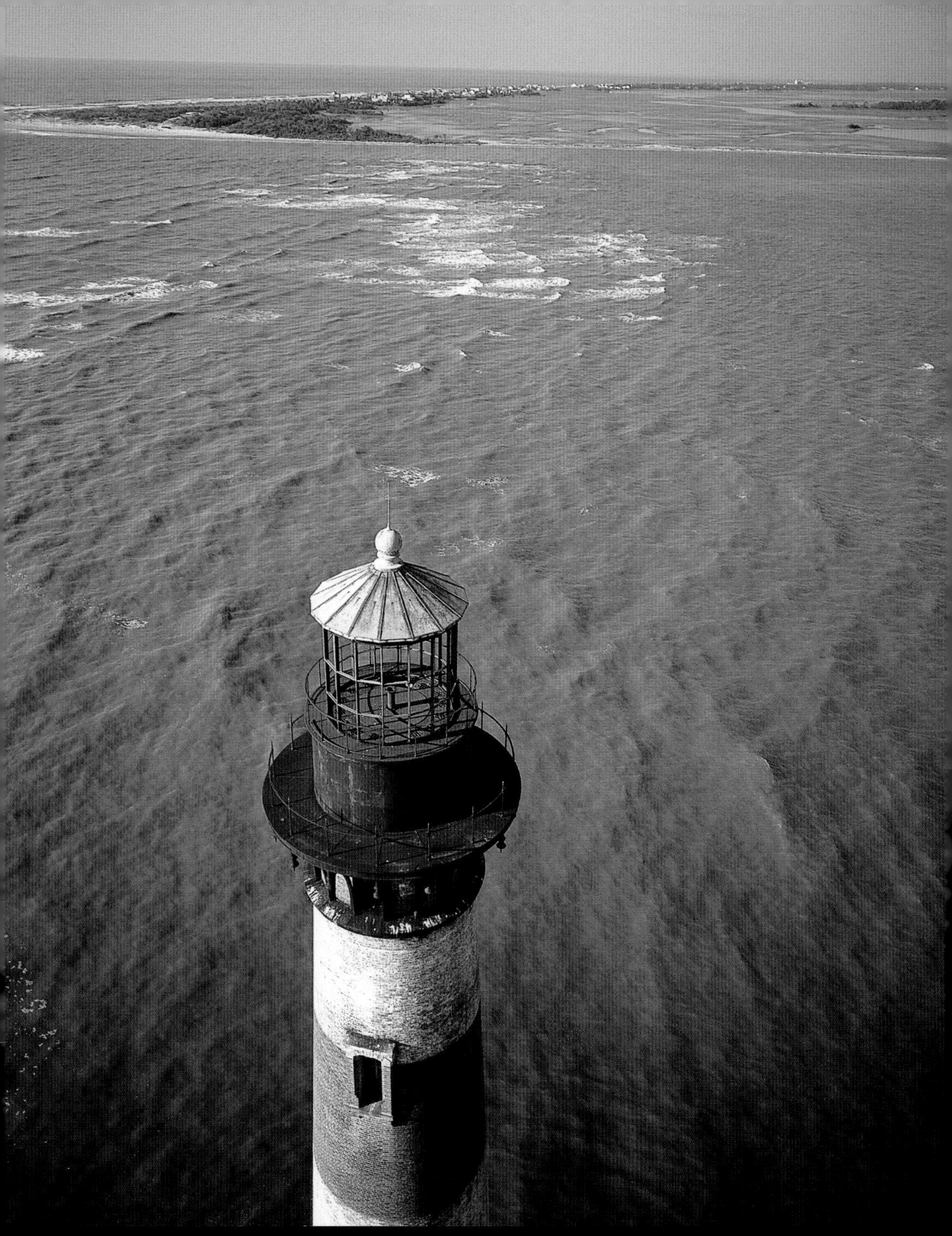

Above: Morris Island Lighthouse.

Left: Tidal marsh, ACE Basin.

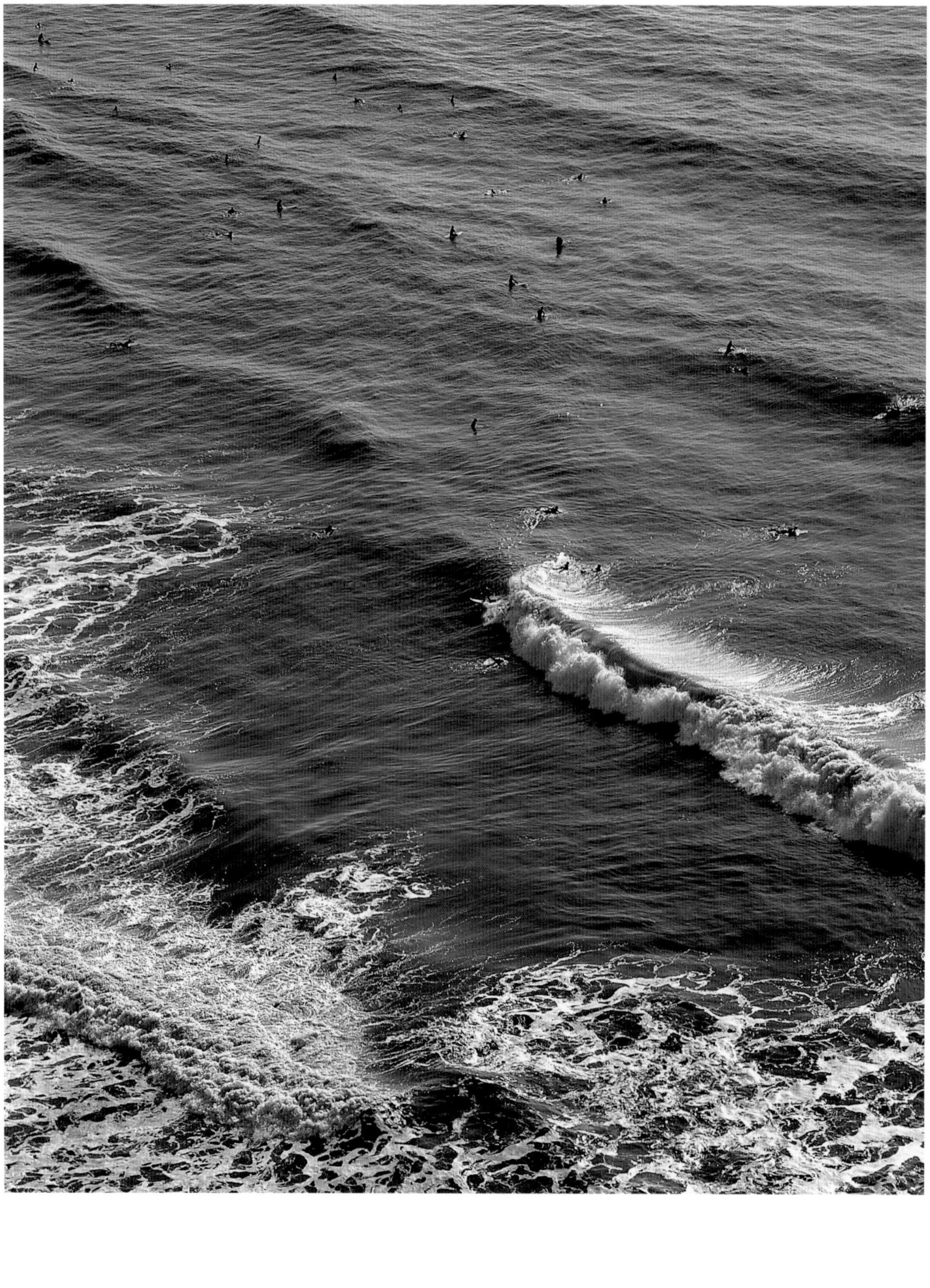

Above and Right: Surfers. Folly Beach.

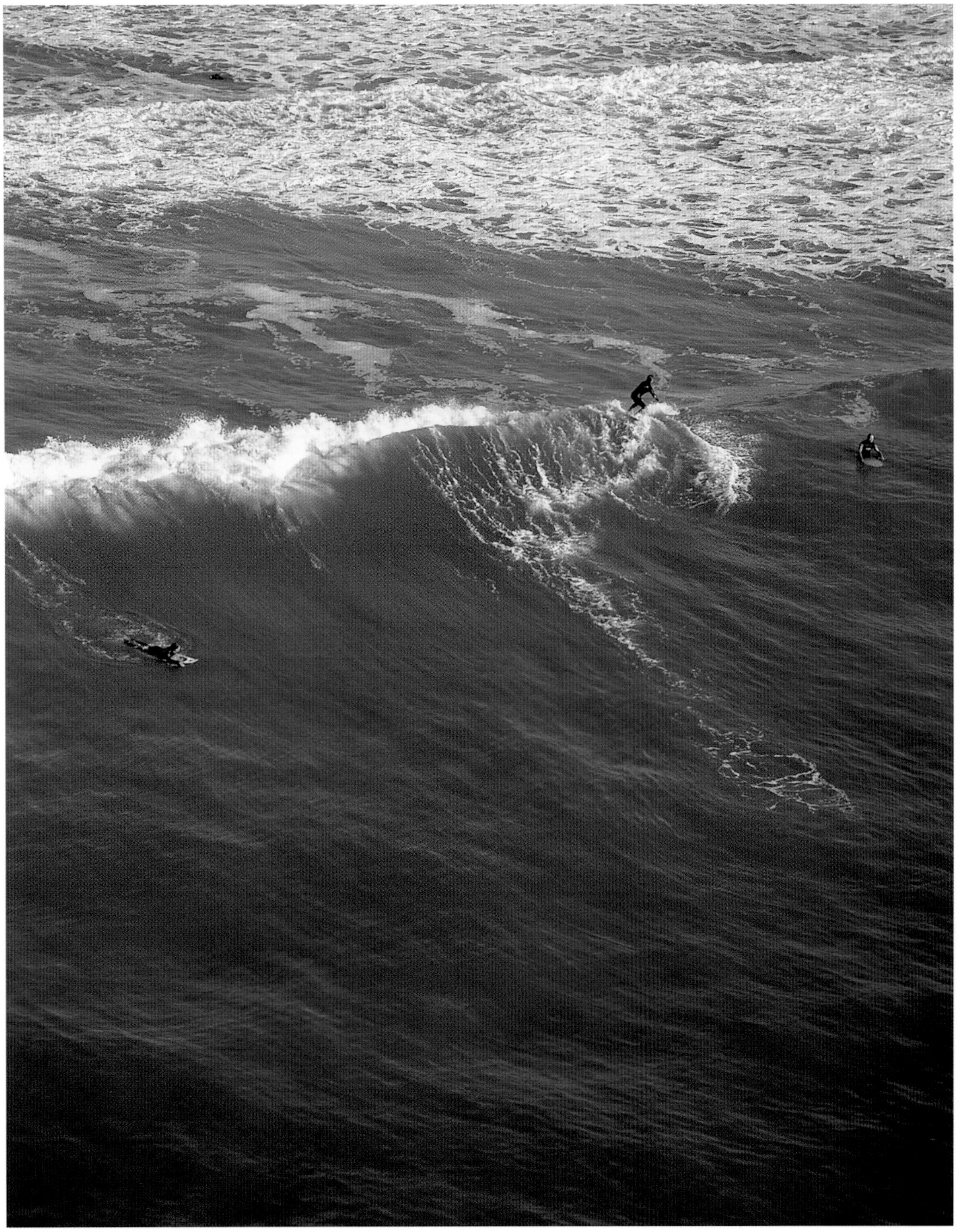

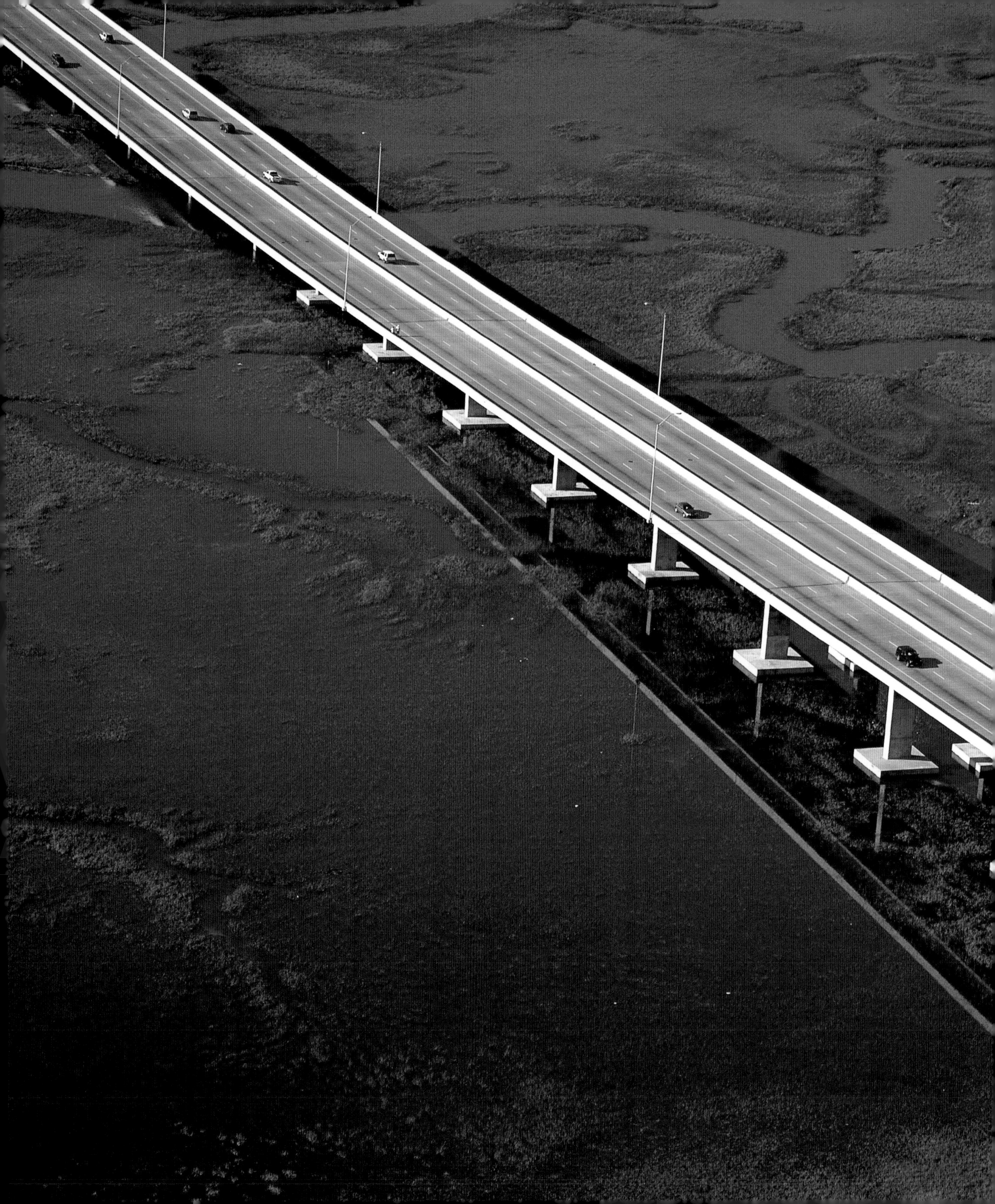

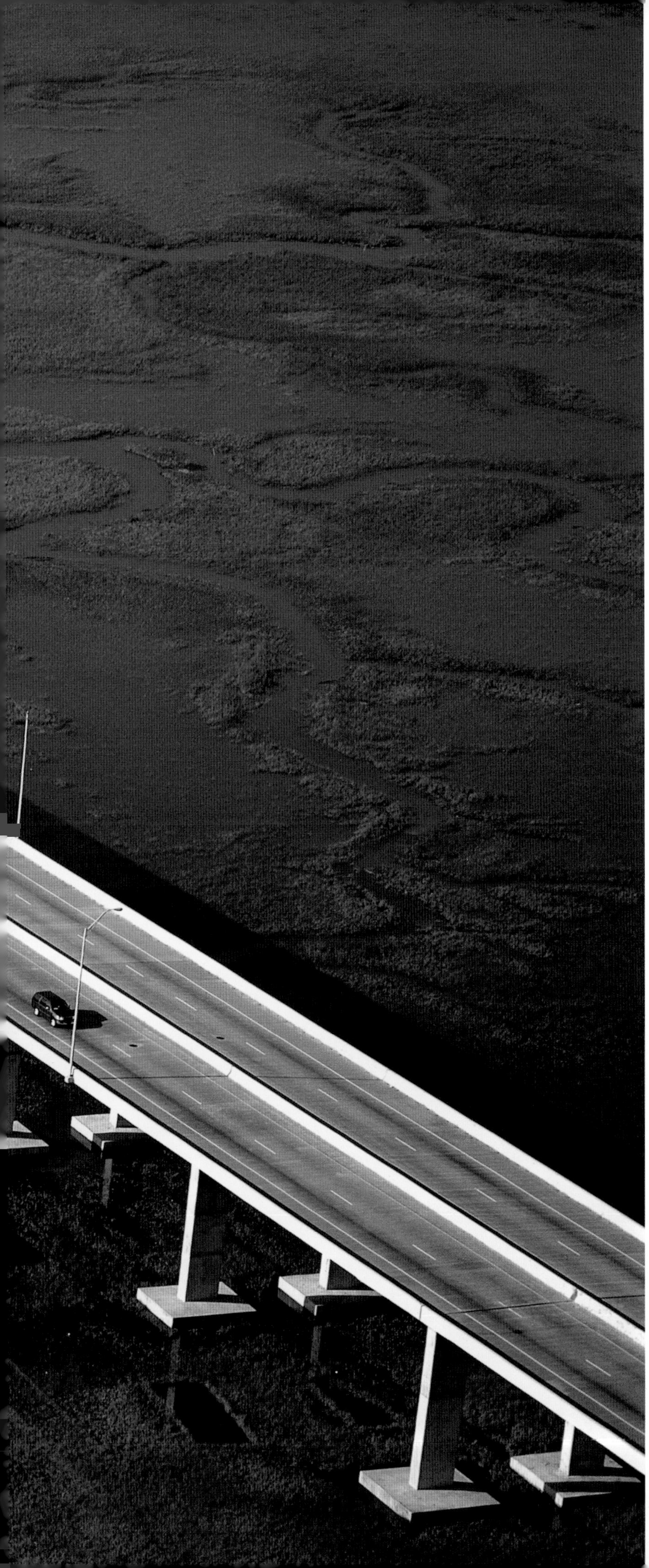

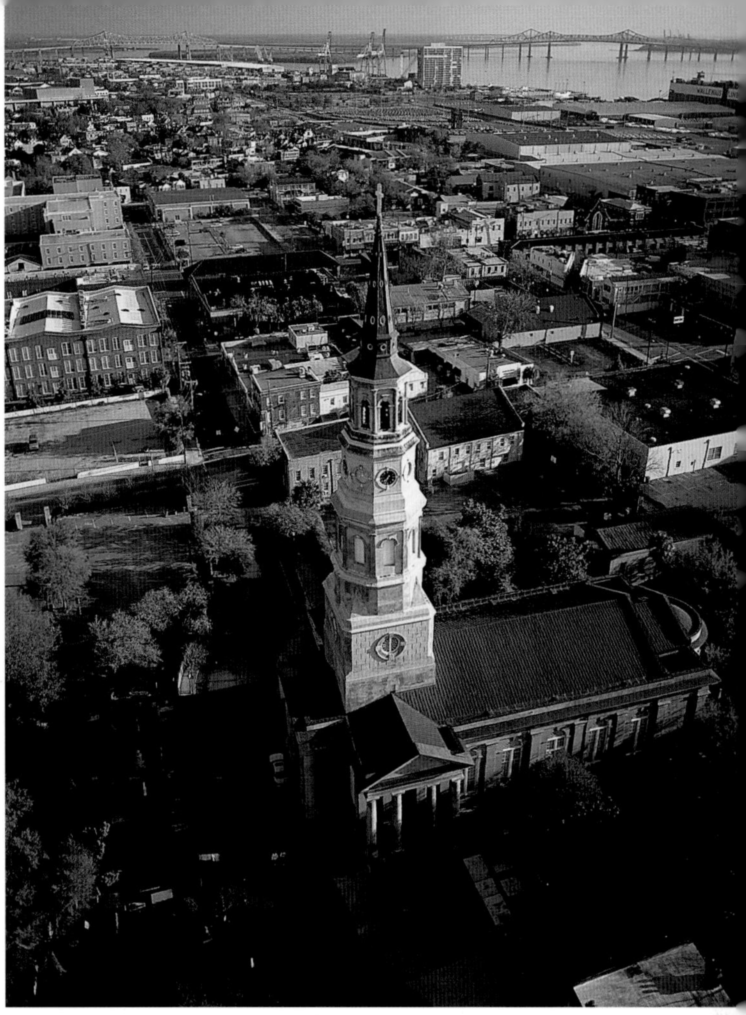

Above: St. Philip's Episcopal Church. Charleston.

Left: Talmadge Memorial Bridge. Savannah.

Next Page: Tidal creek. Beaufort County.

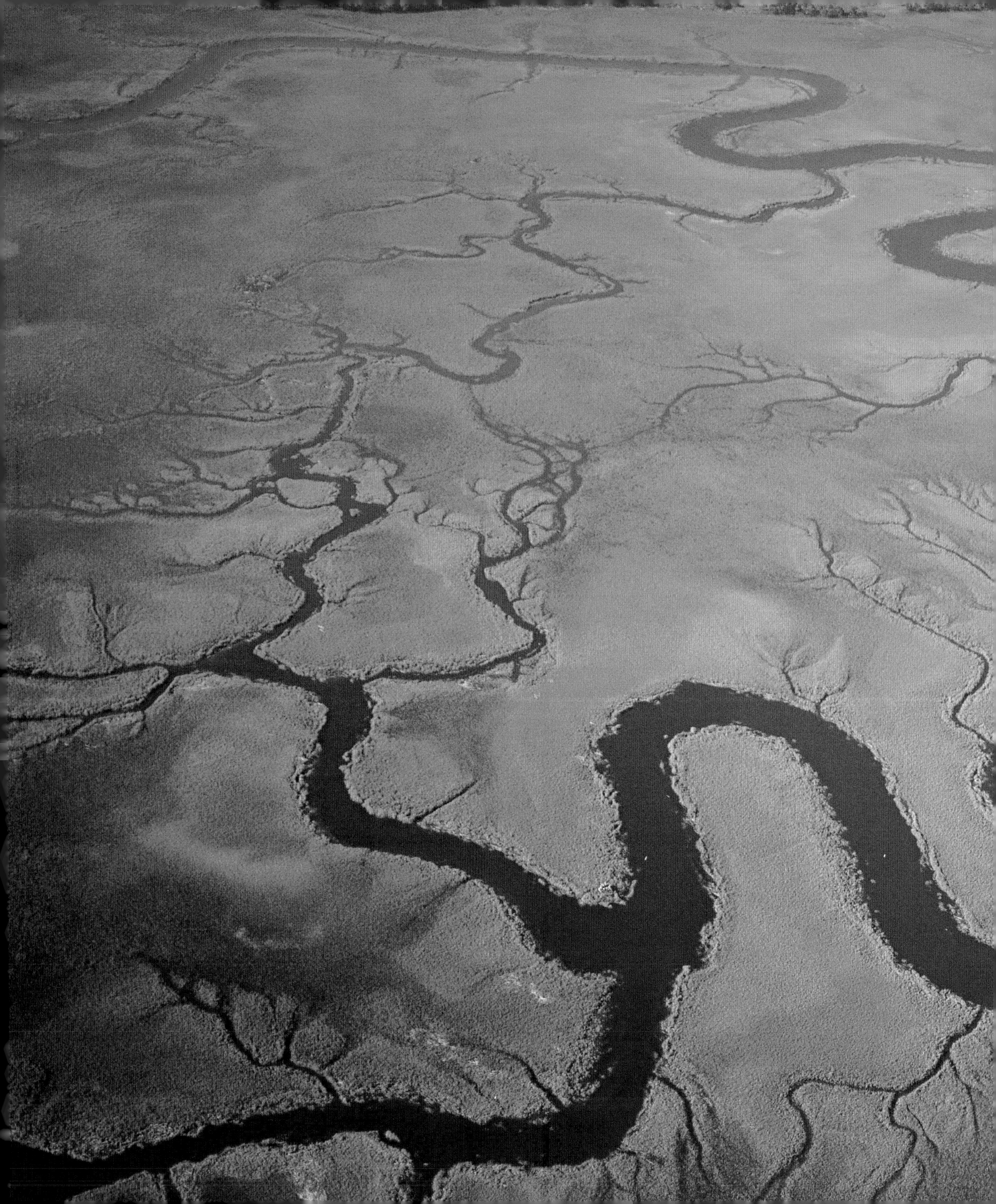

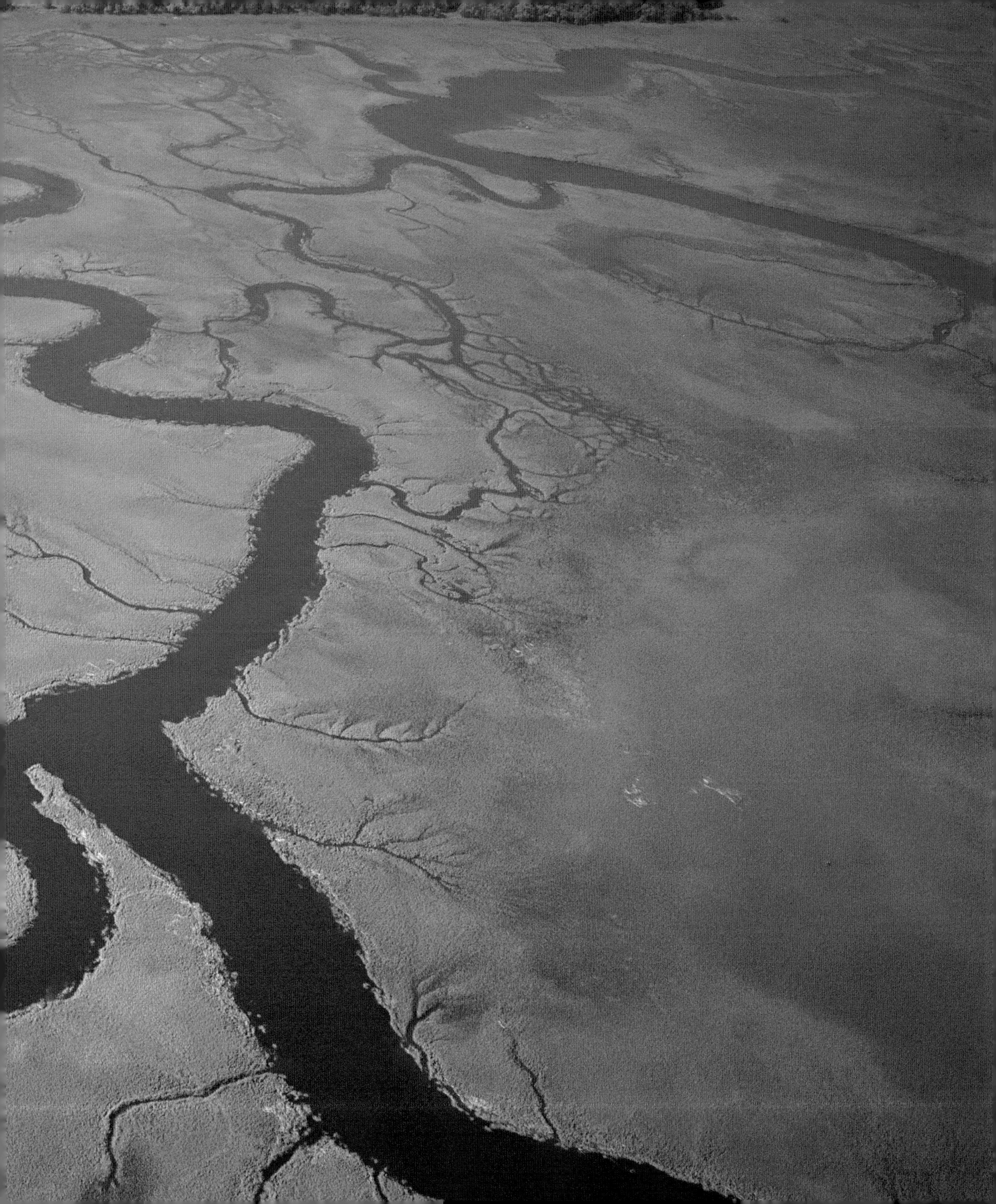

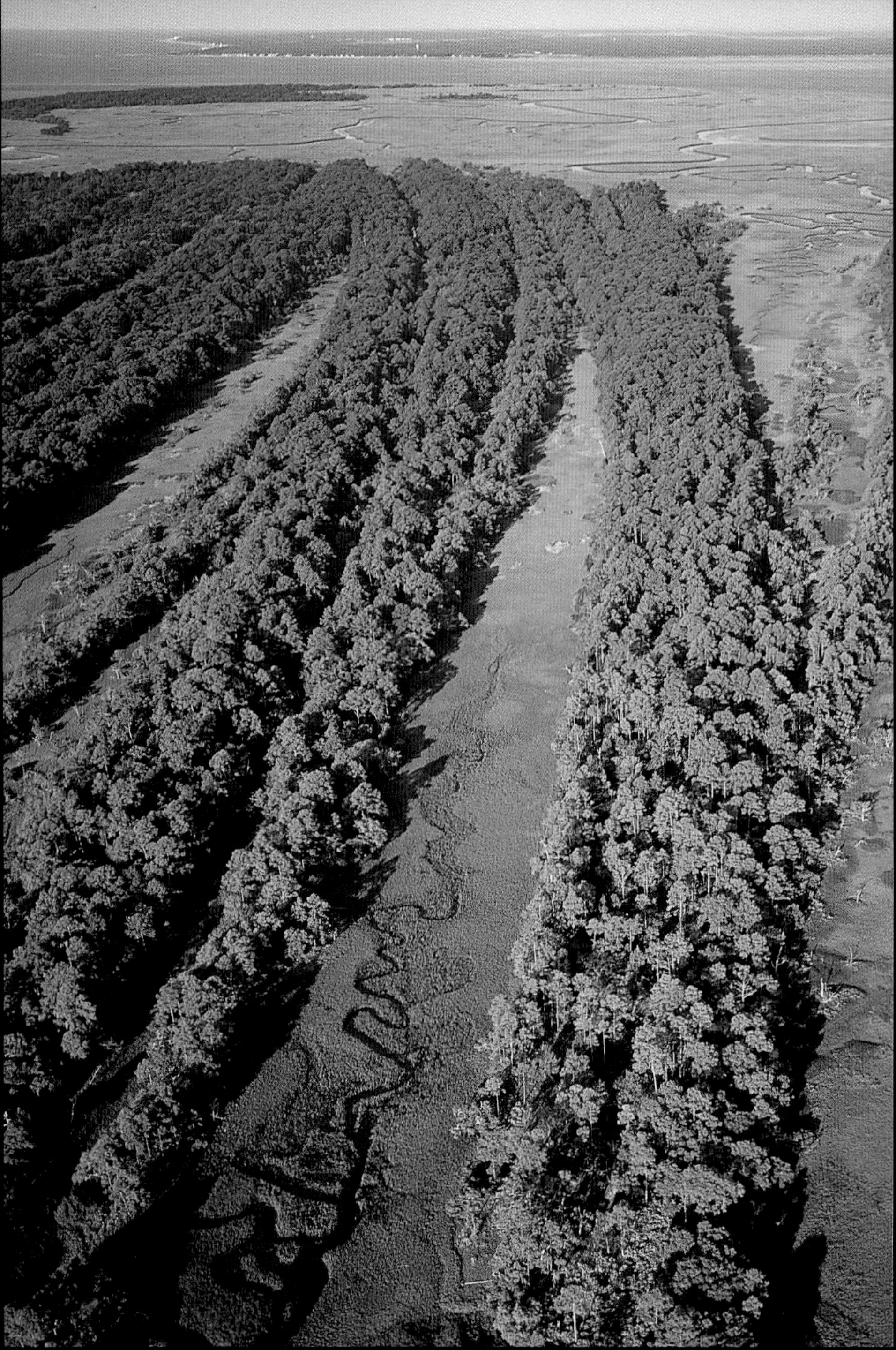

Above: St. Phillips Island. Hilton Head.

Right: Sand banks. Fripp Inlet.

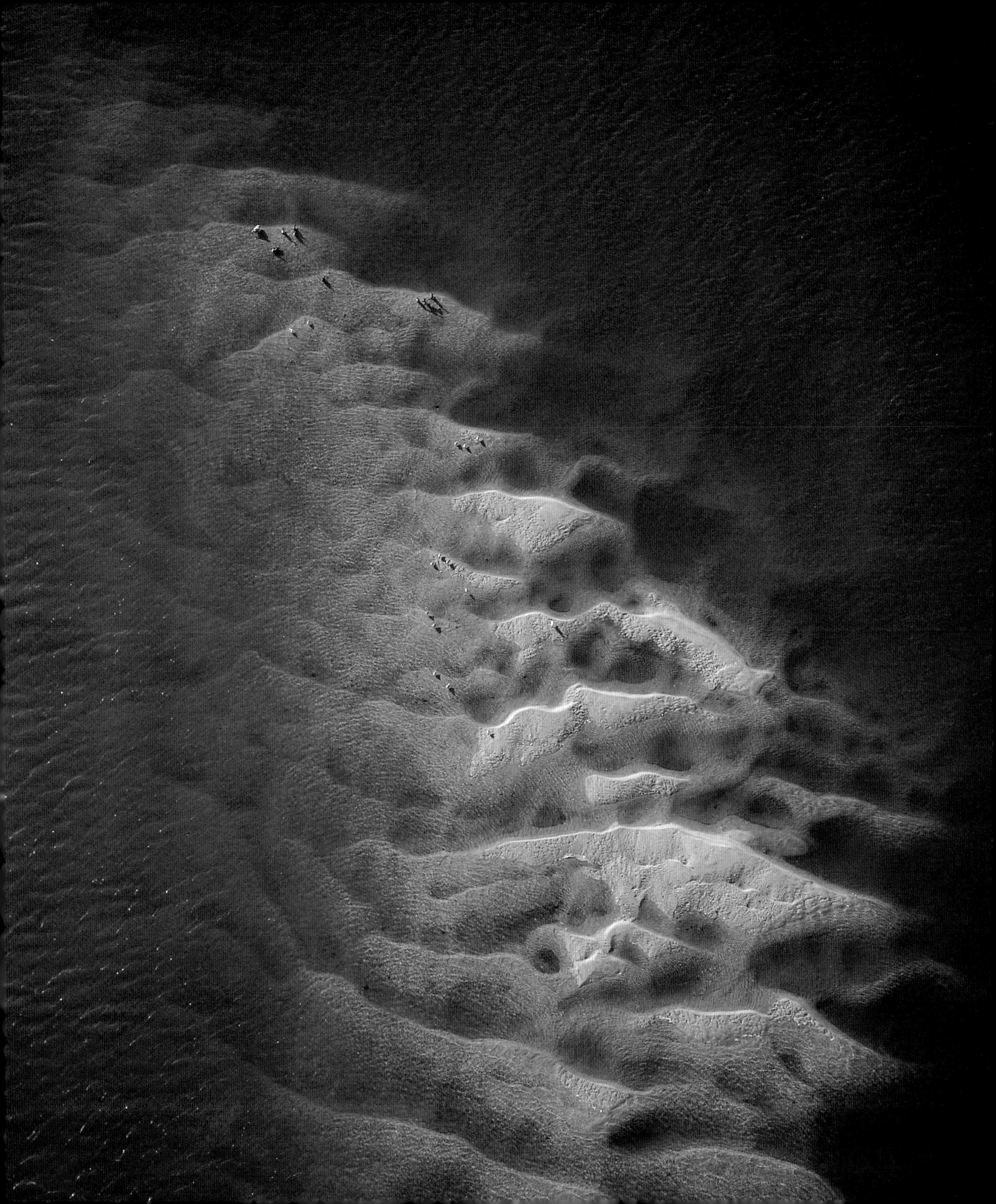

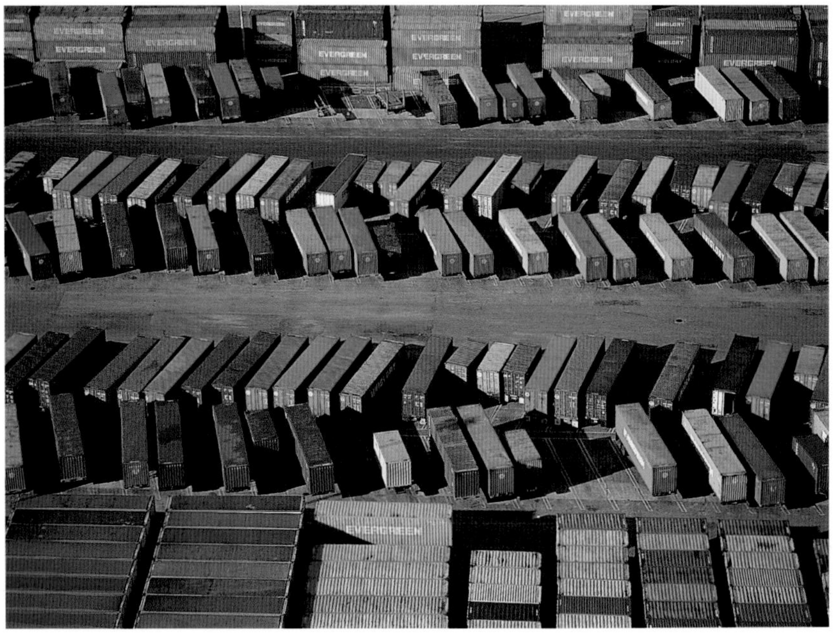

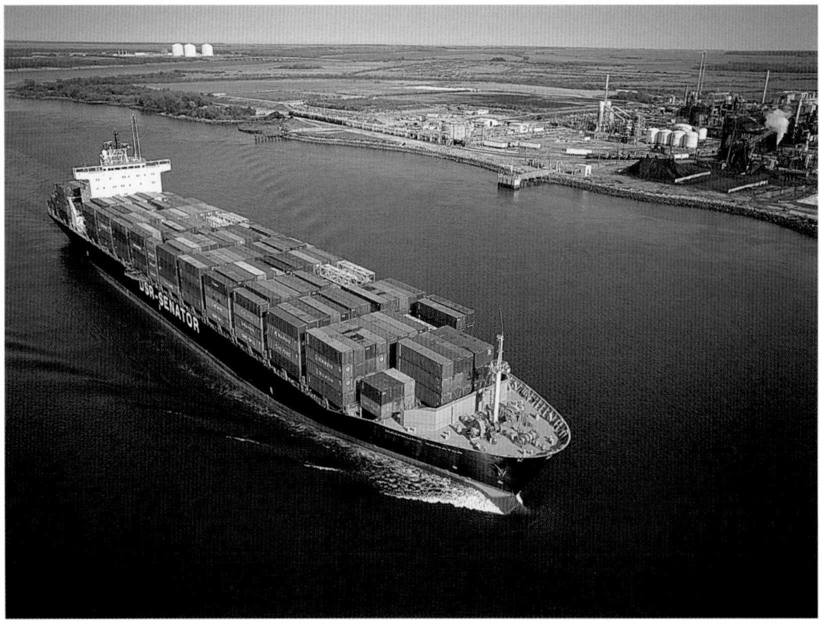

Top: Containers at dock. Savannah.

Bottom: Container ship. Savannah.

Right: Low tide. Stono Inlet.

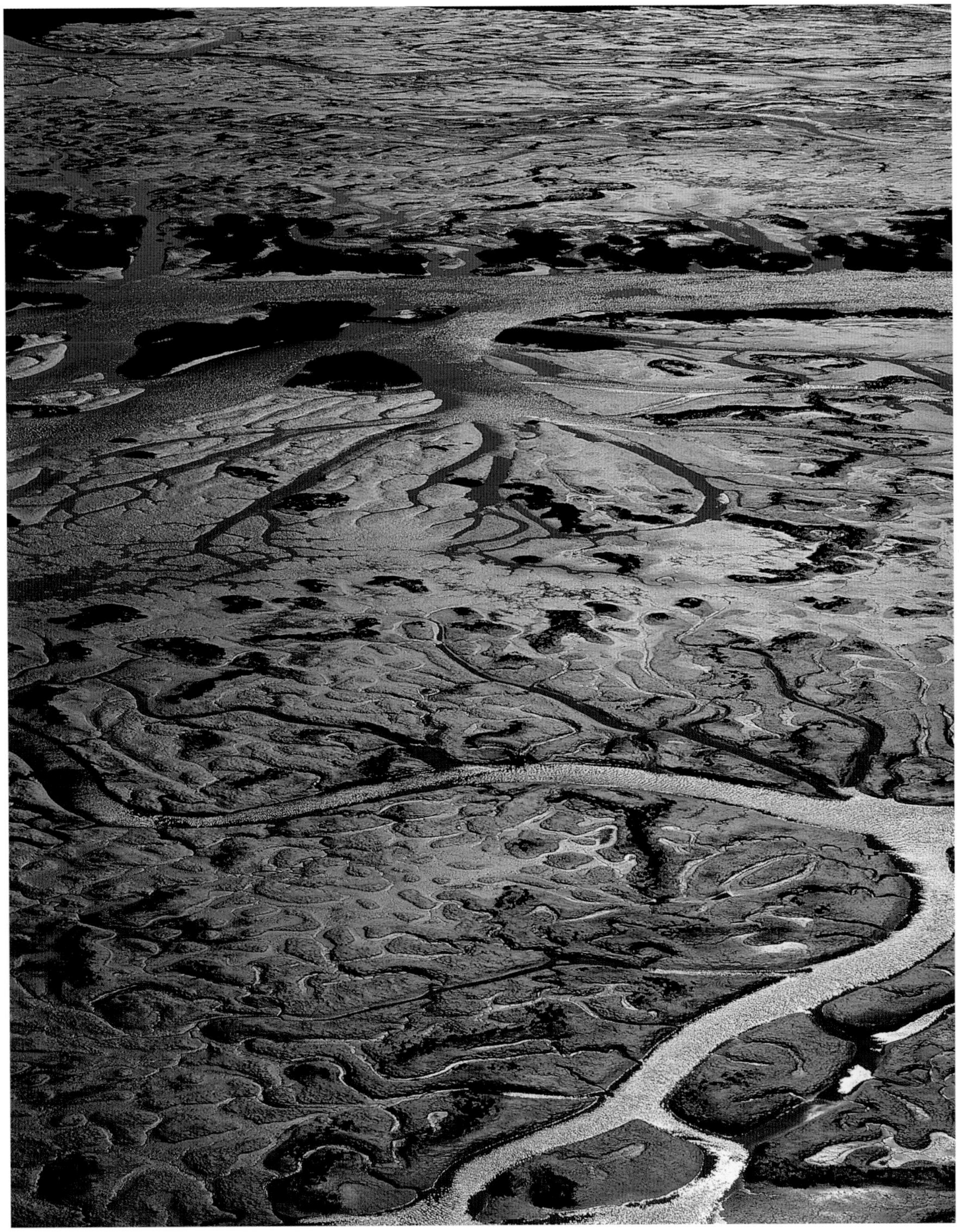

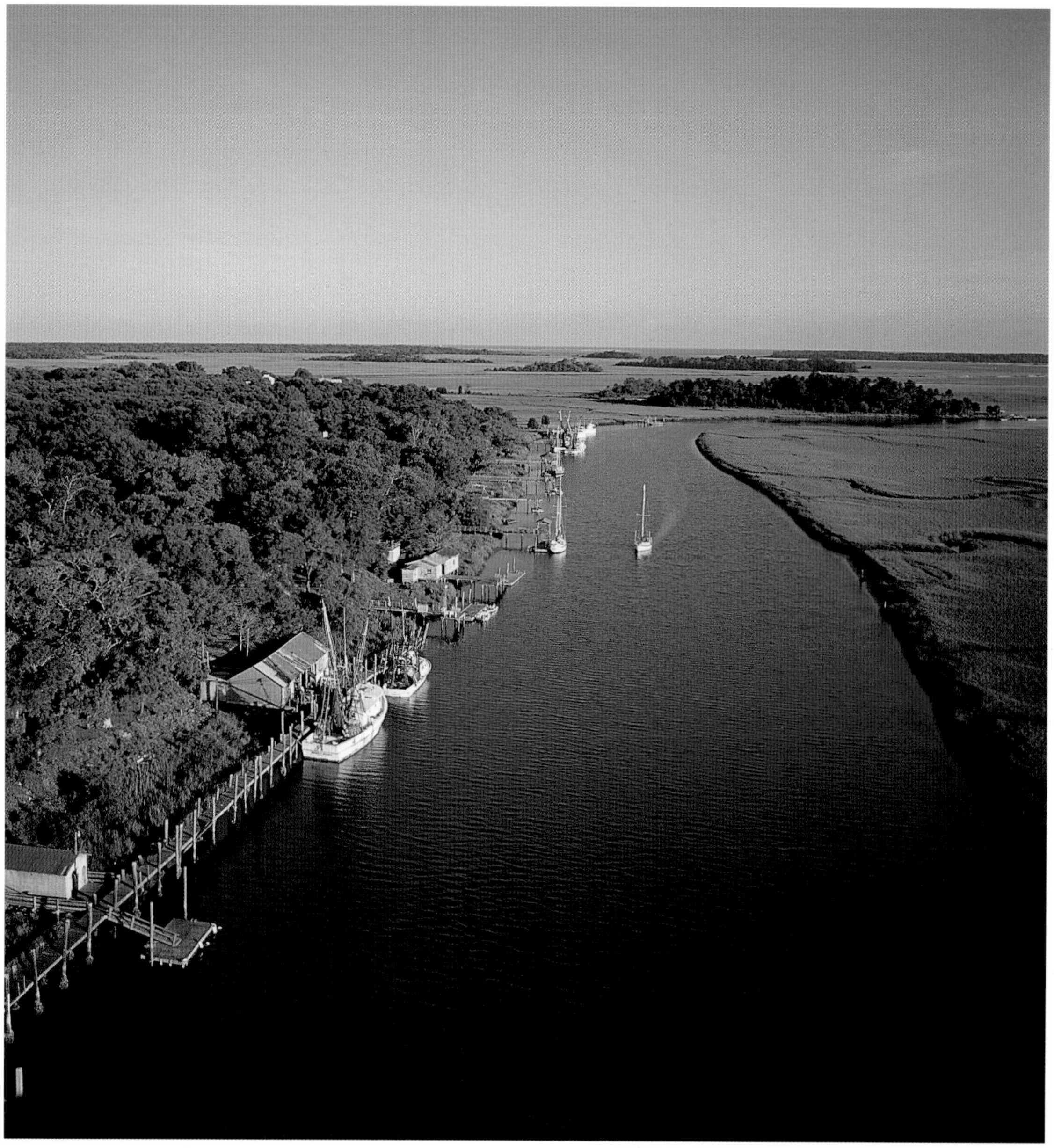

Above: Rockville.

Right: Tidal creek. Daufuskie Island.

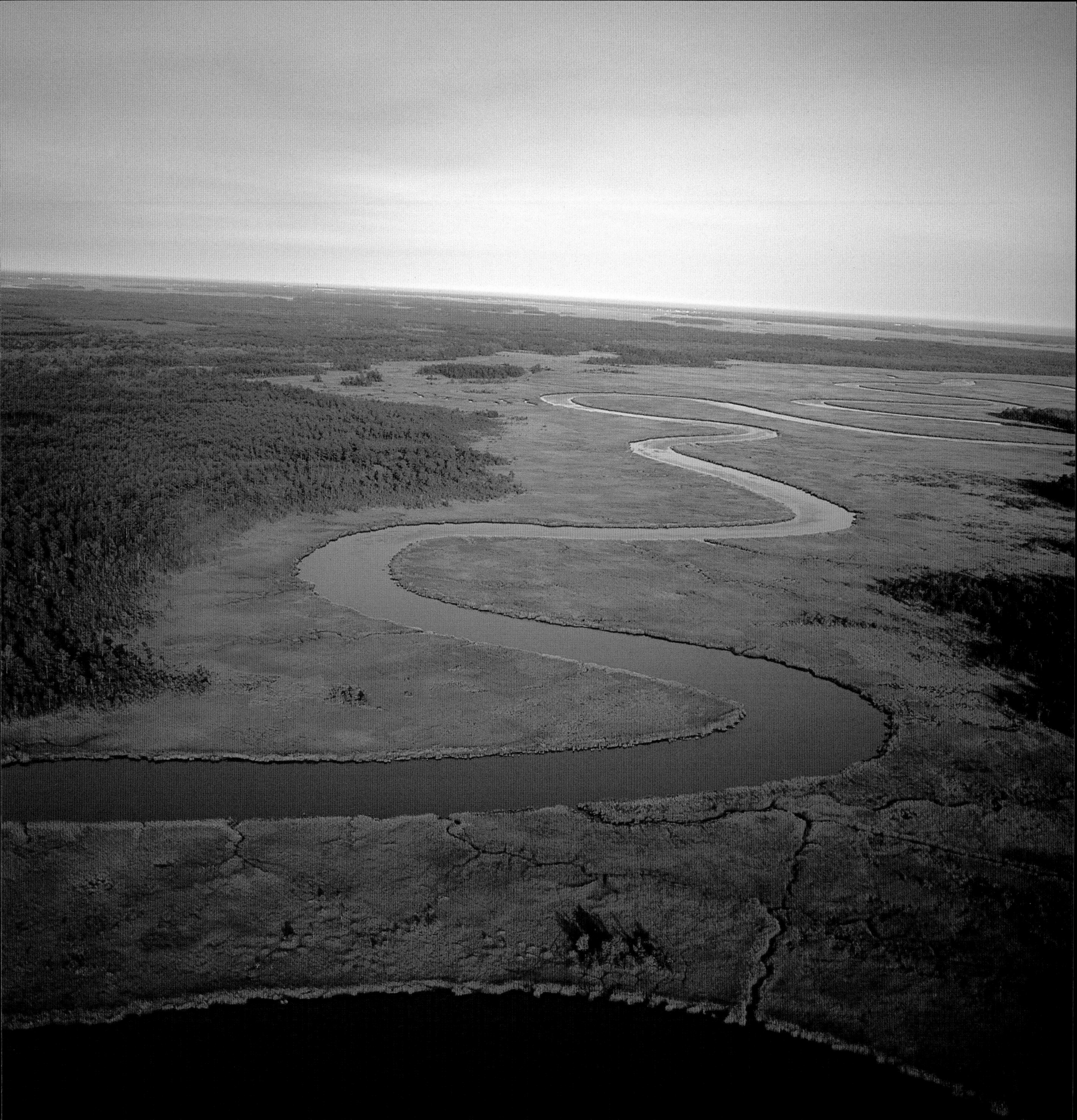

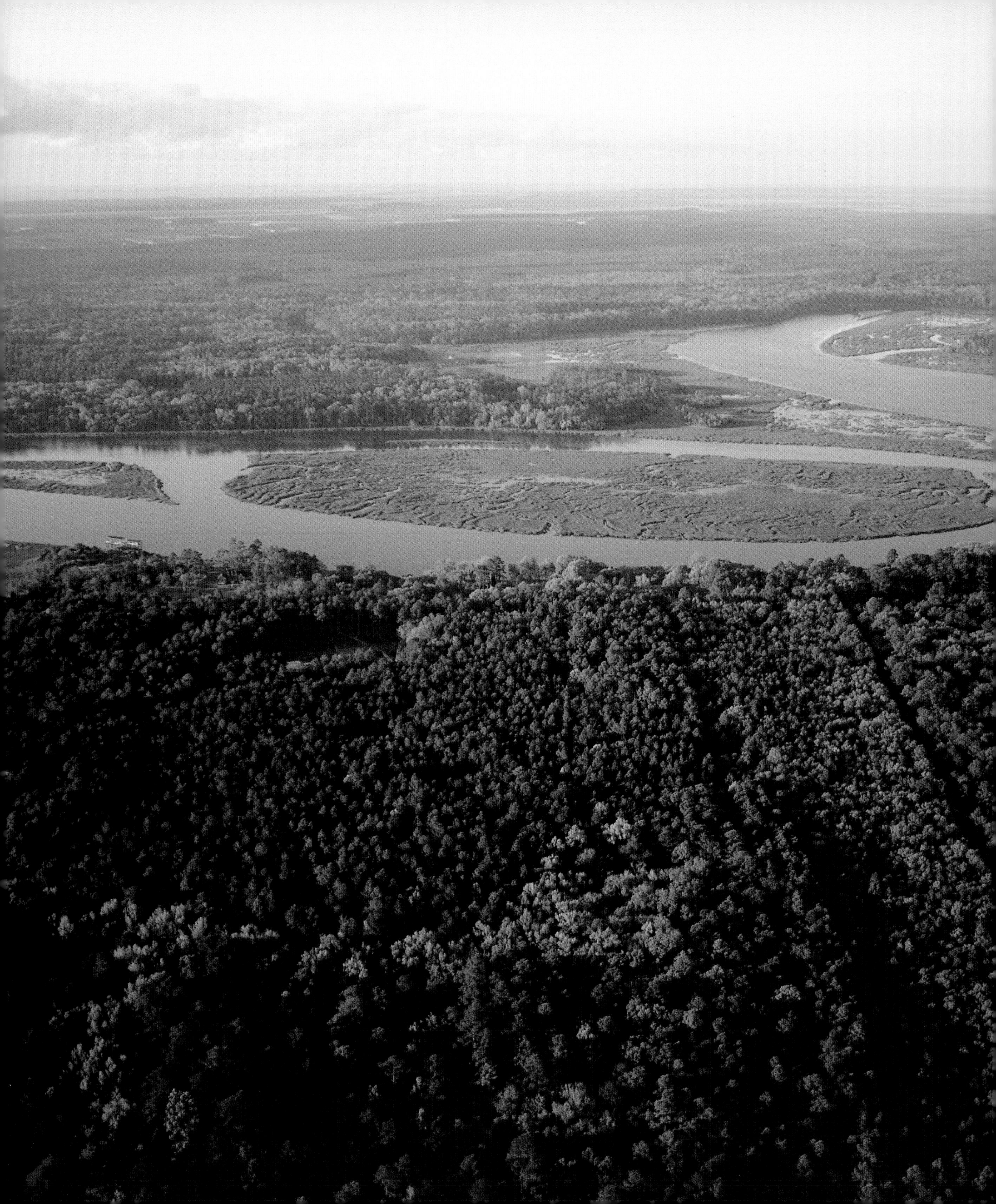

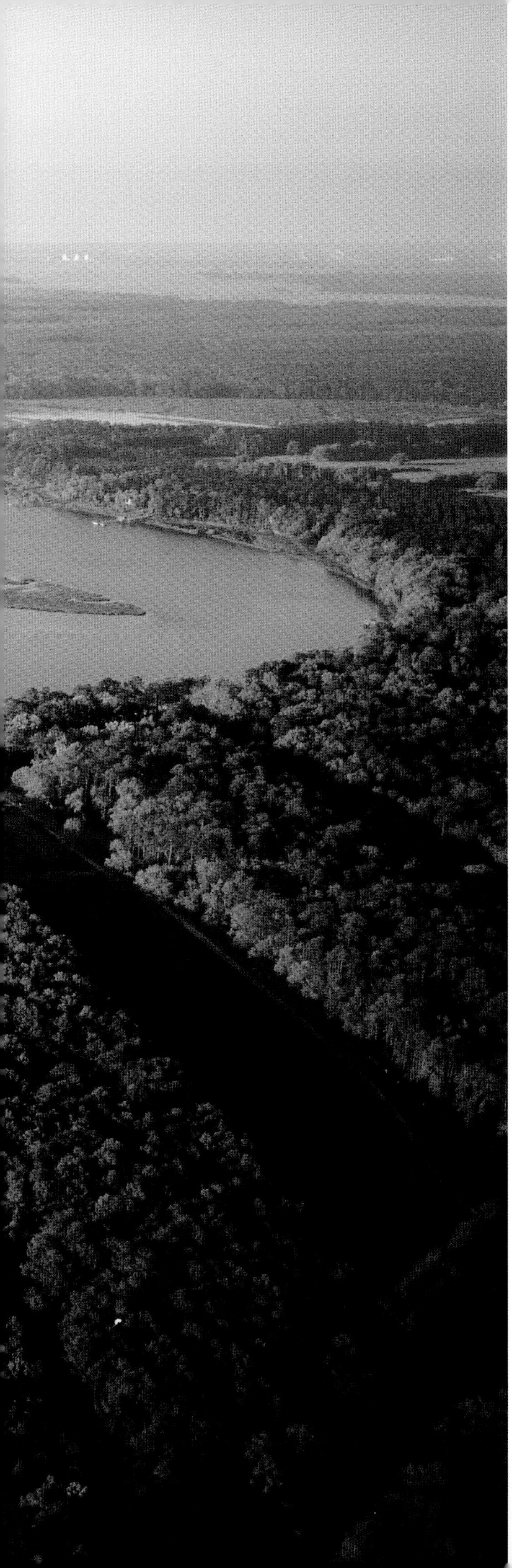

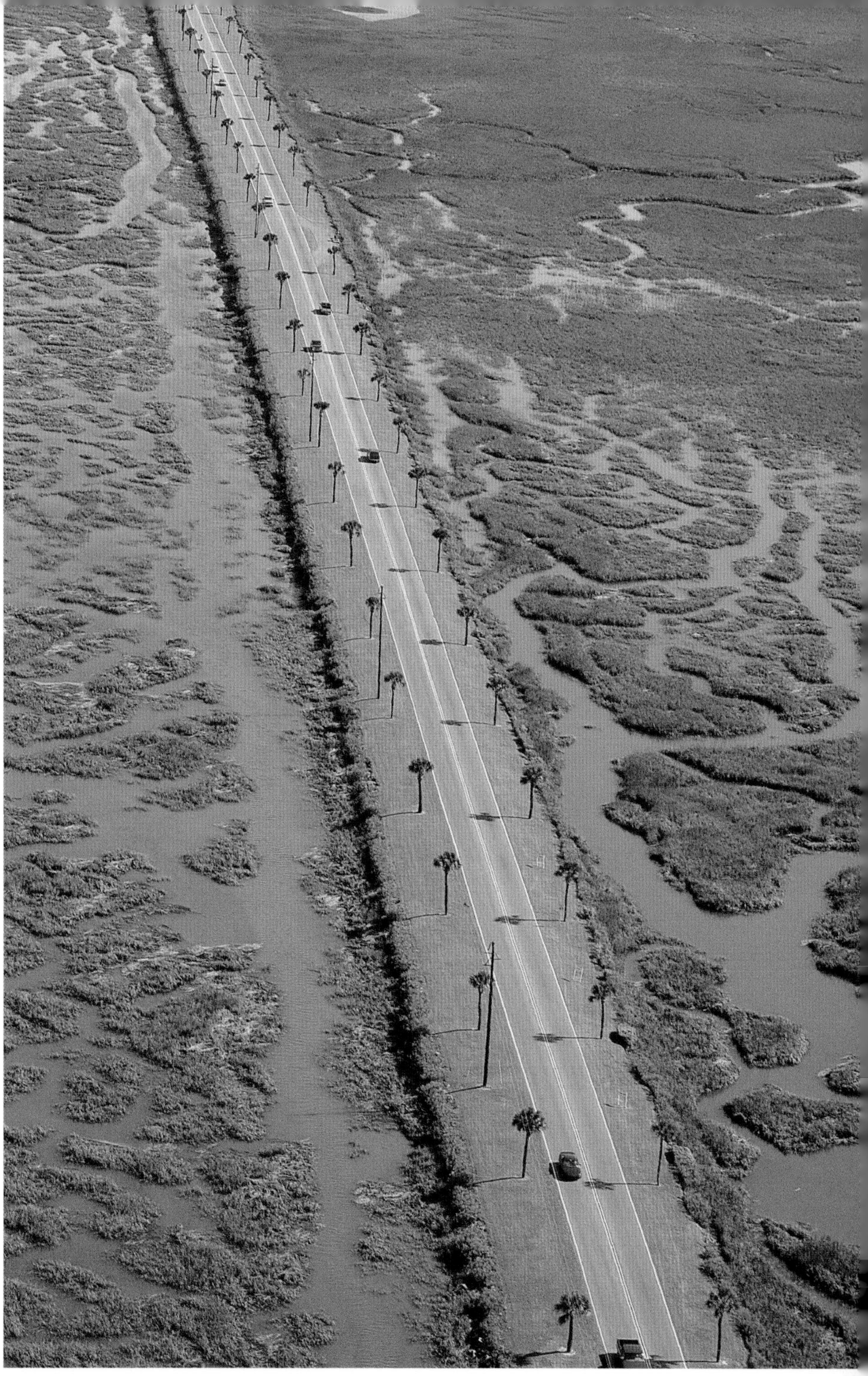

Above: Causeway to Parris Island.

Left: Near Daufuskie Island.

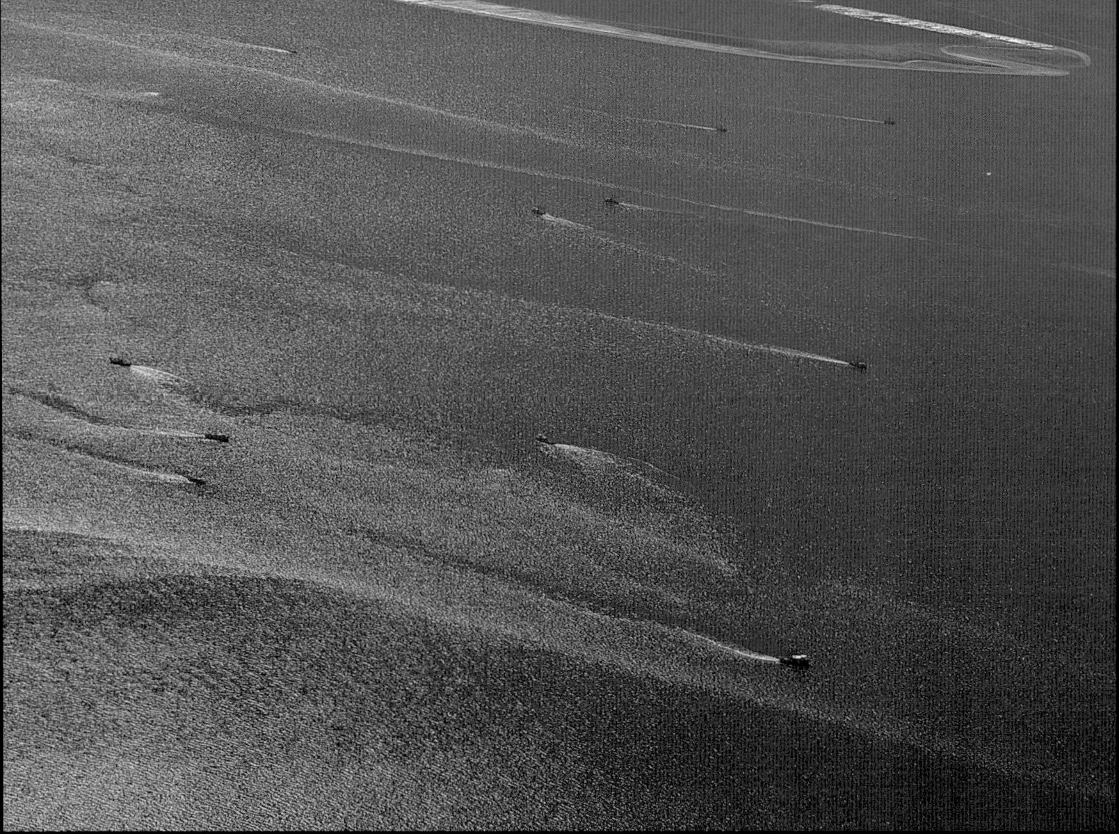

Above: Shrimp boats. Beaufort River.

Right: Pier at Folly Beach.

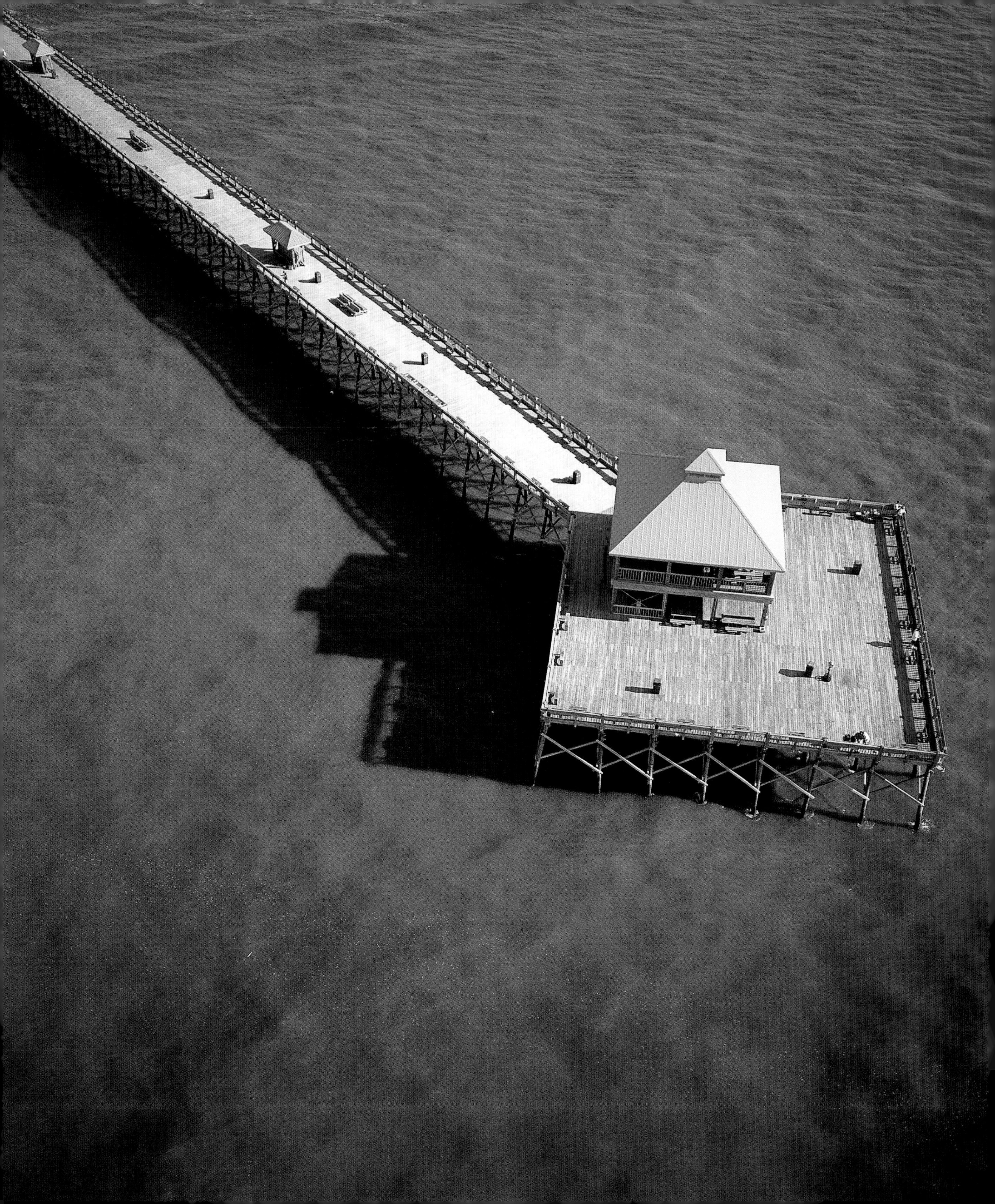

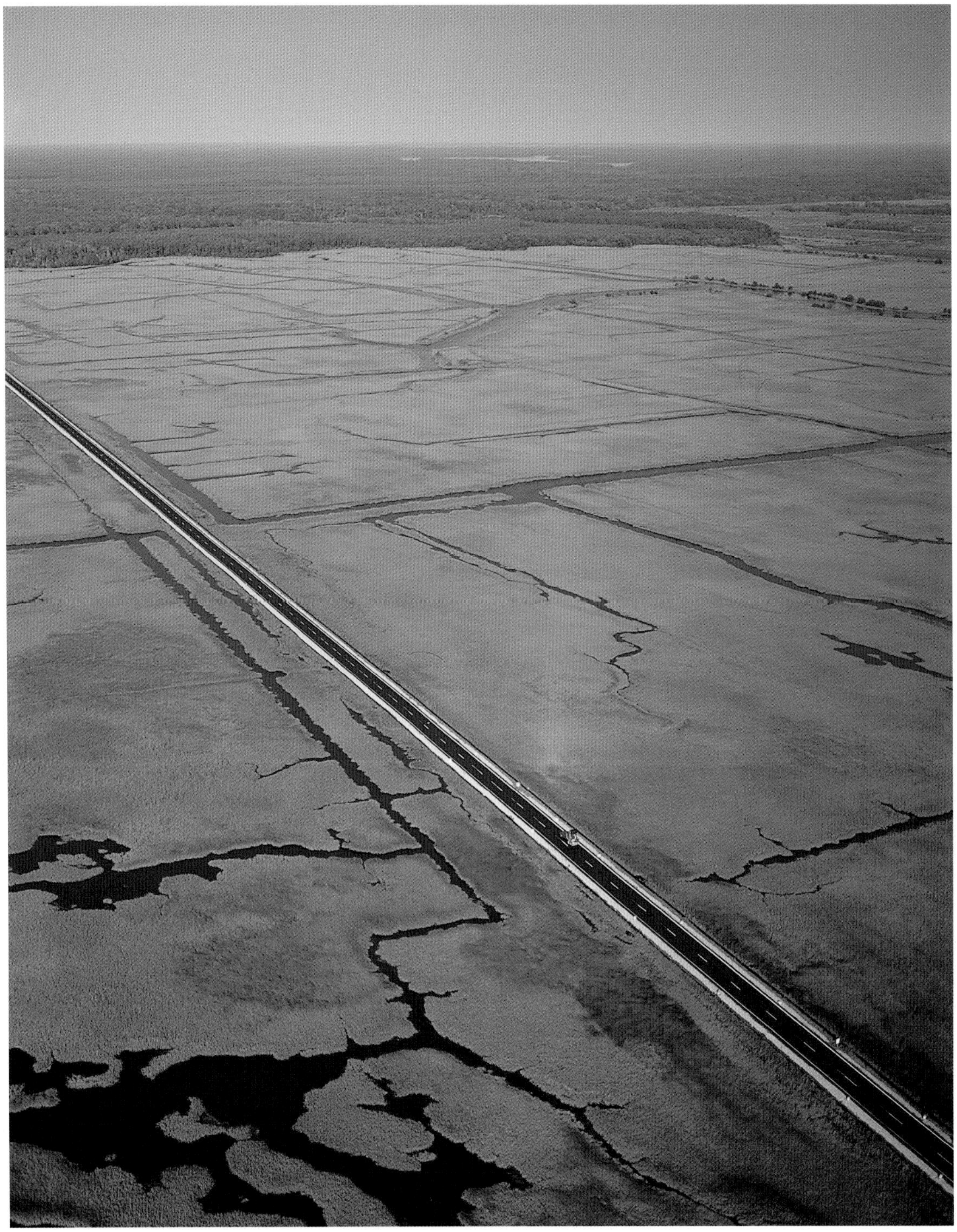

Above: Highway 17. ACE Basin.

Right: Near Daufuskie Island.

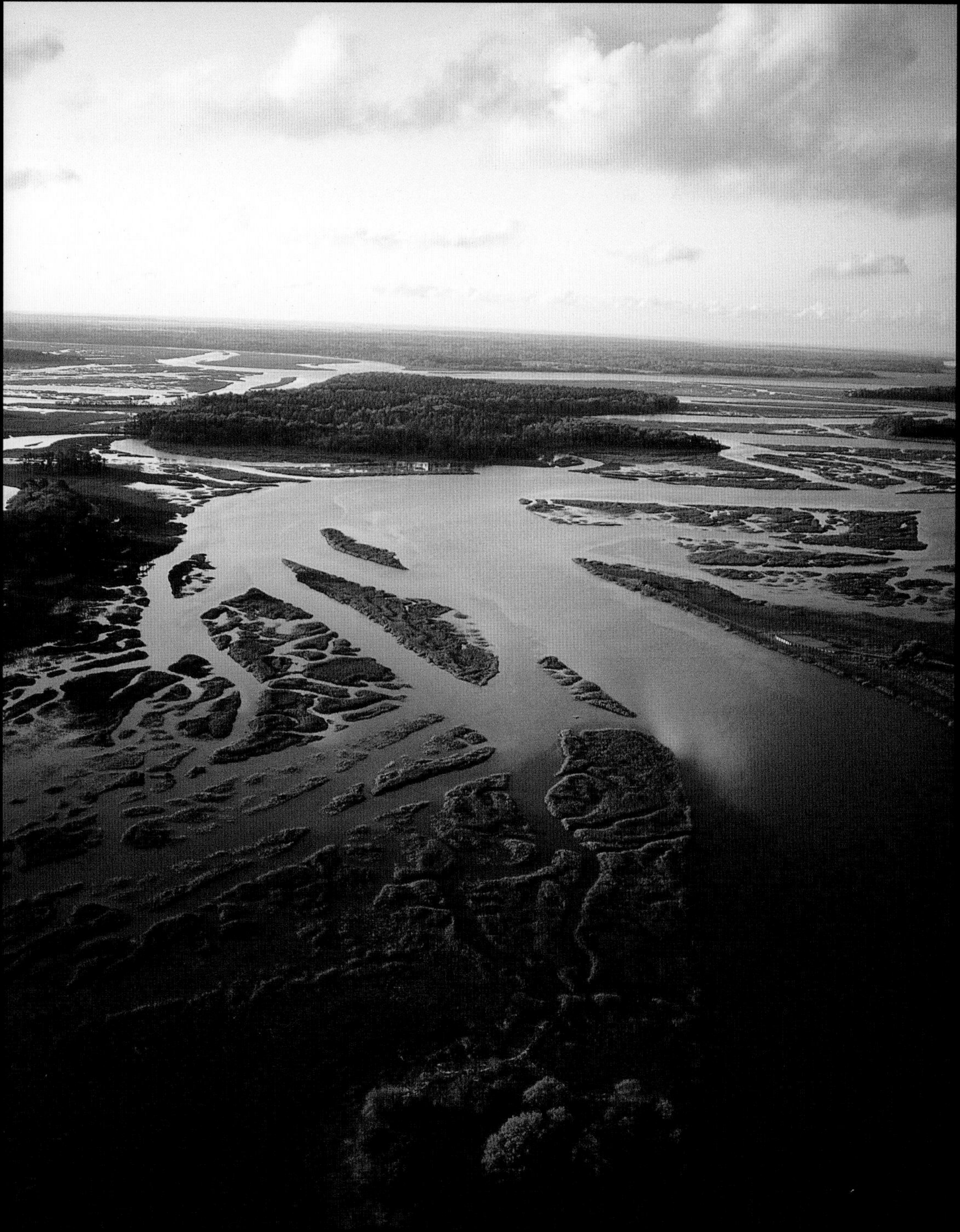

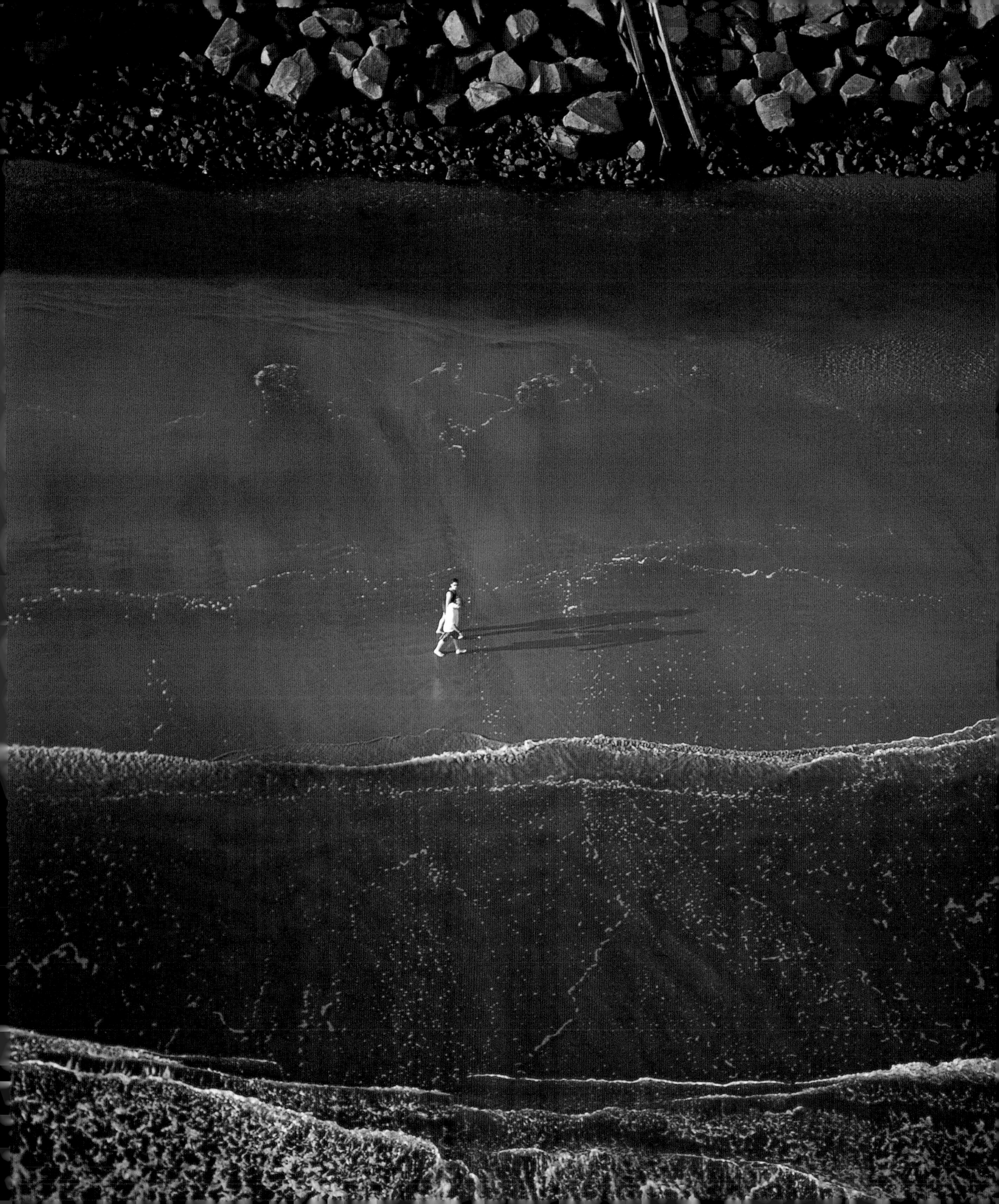

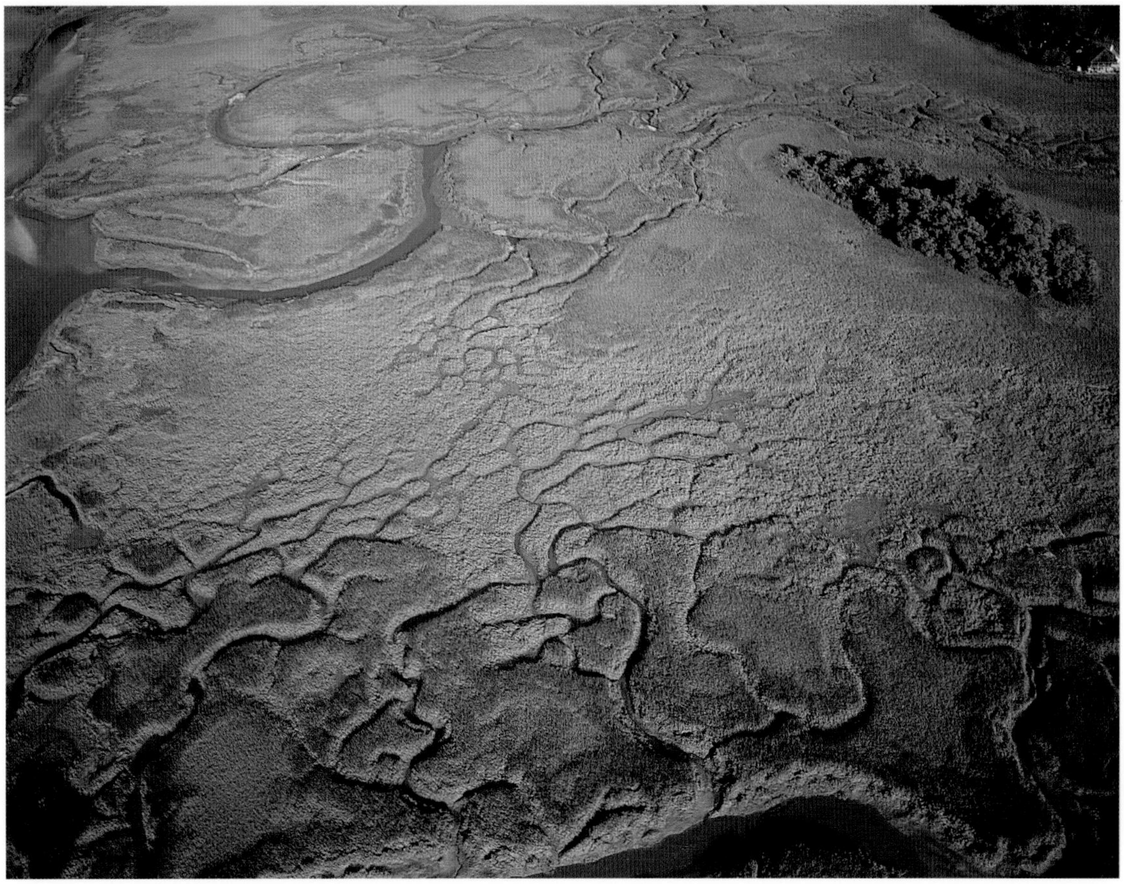

Above: Broad Creek. Hilton Head Island.

Left: Couple walking on Fripp Island beach

Next Page: Dock. Hilton Head Island.

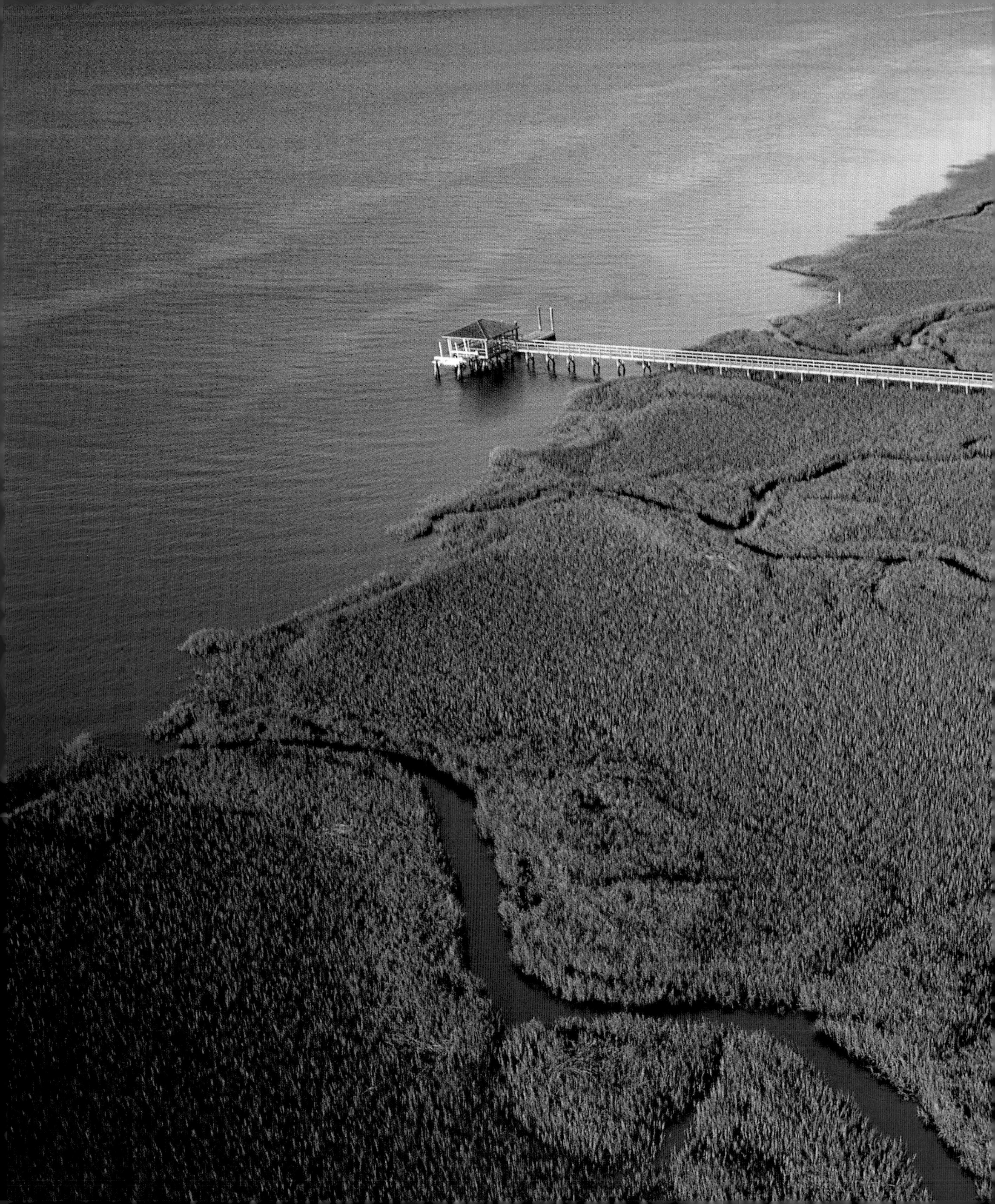

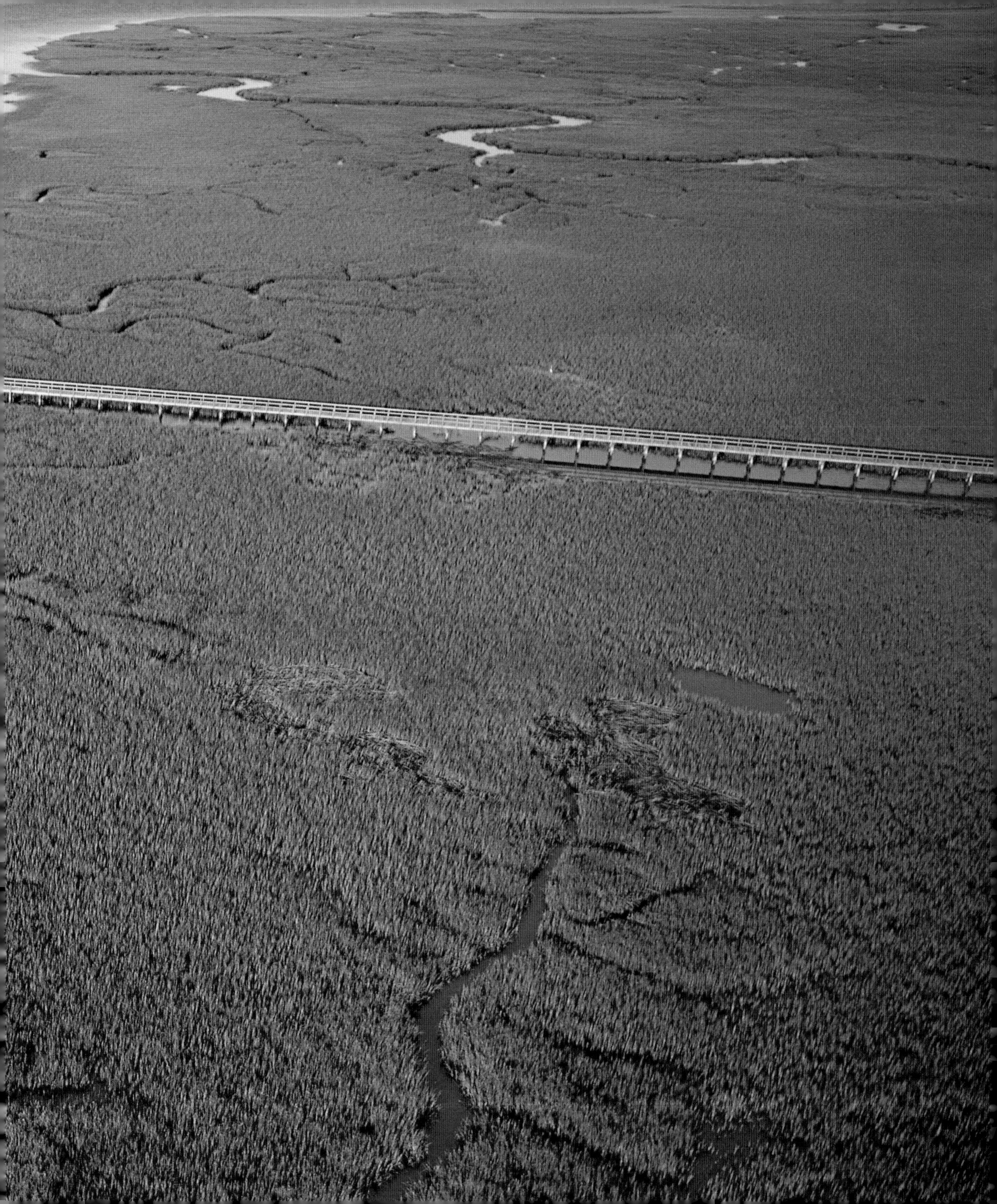

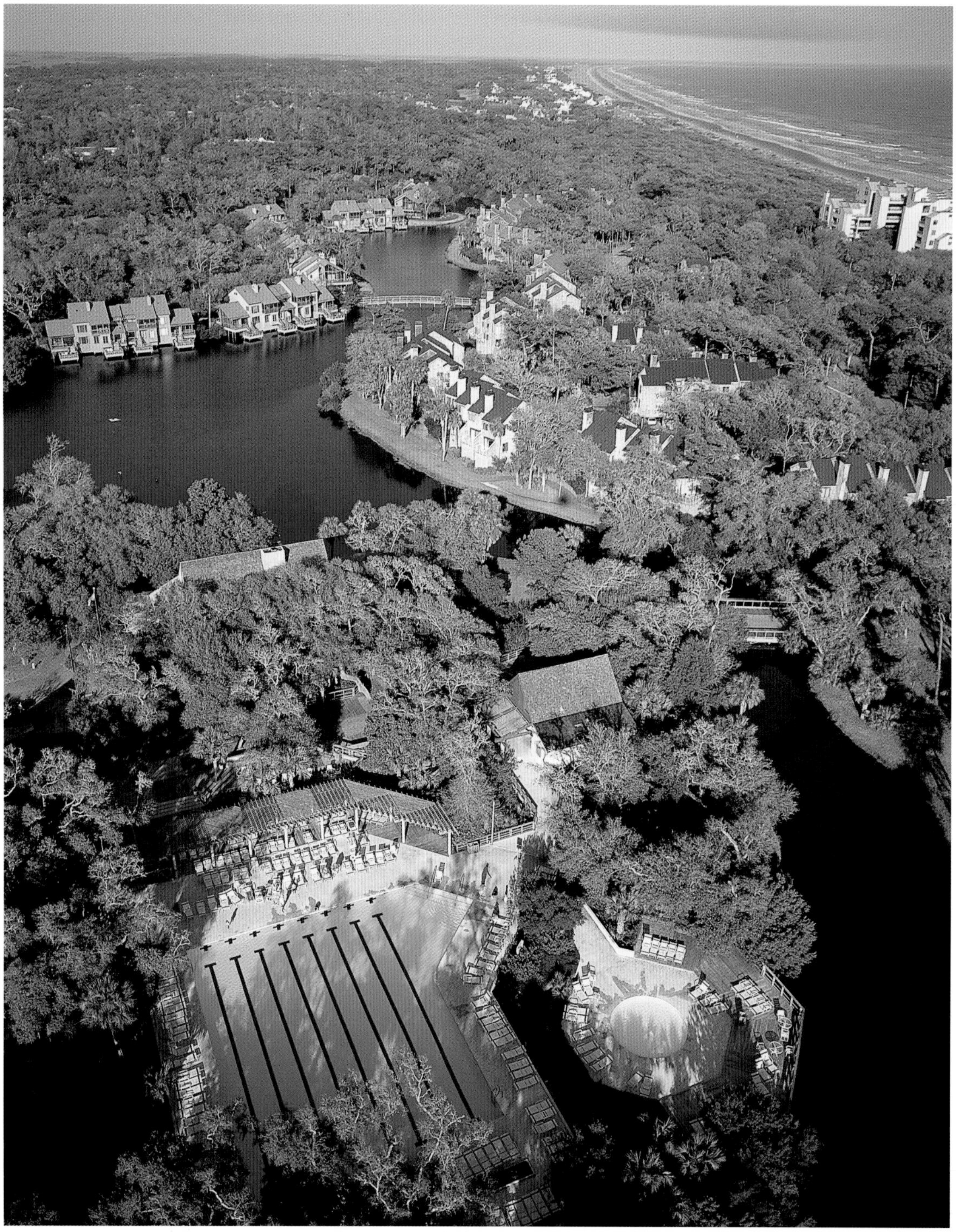

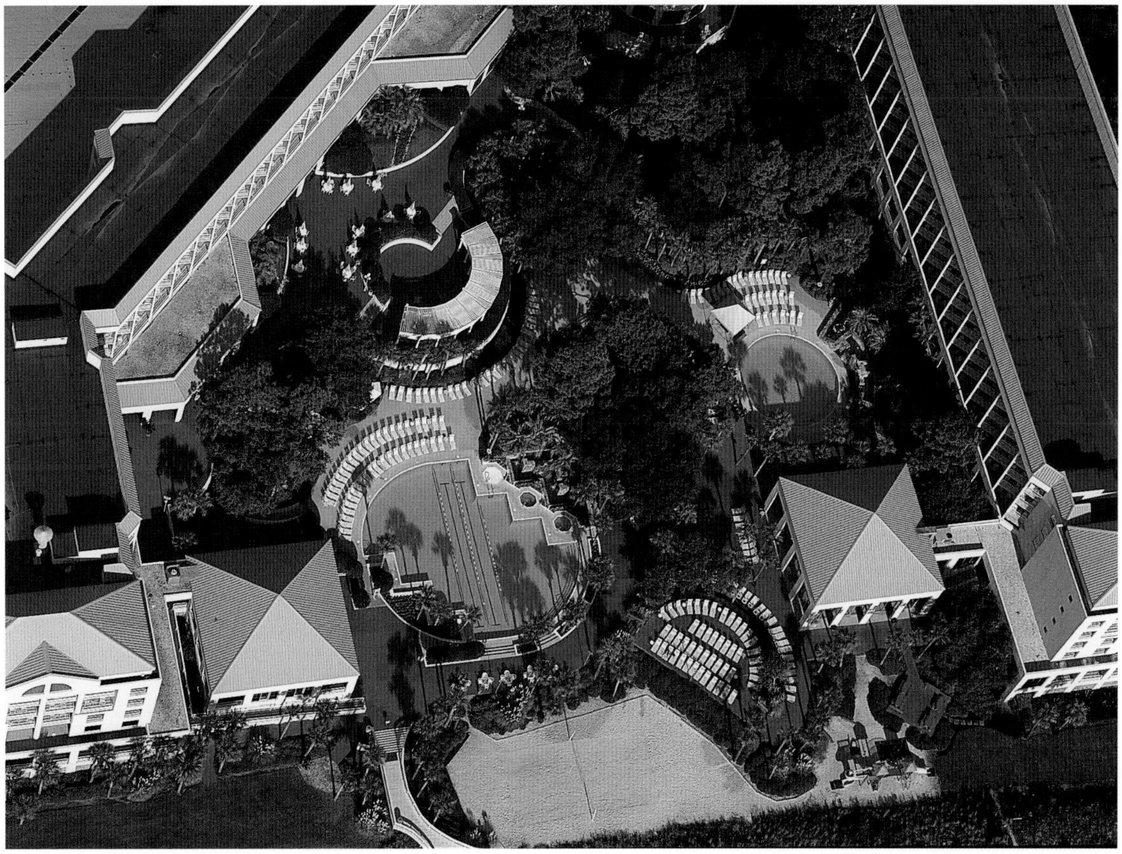

Above: Hotel. Hilton Head Island.

Left: Hilton Head Island.

Next Page: Waterways and creeks. St. Helena Island.

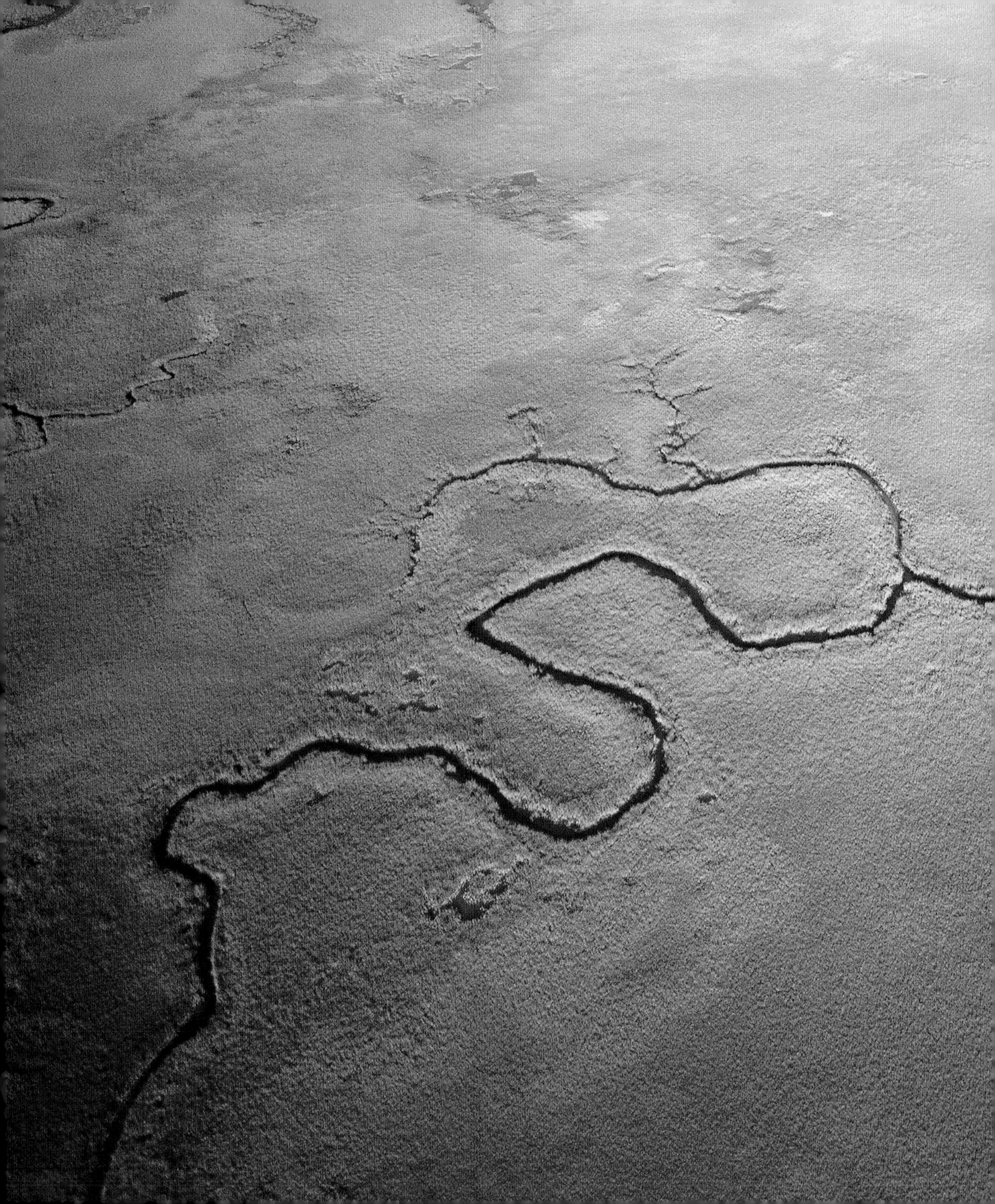

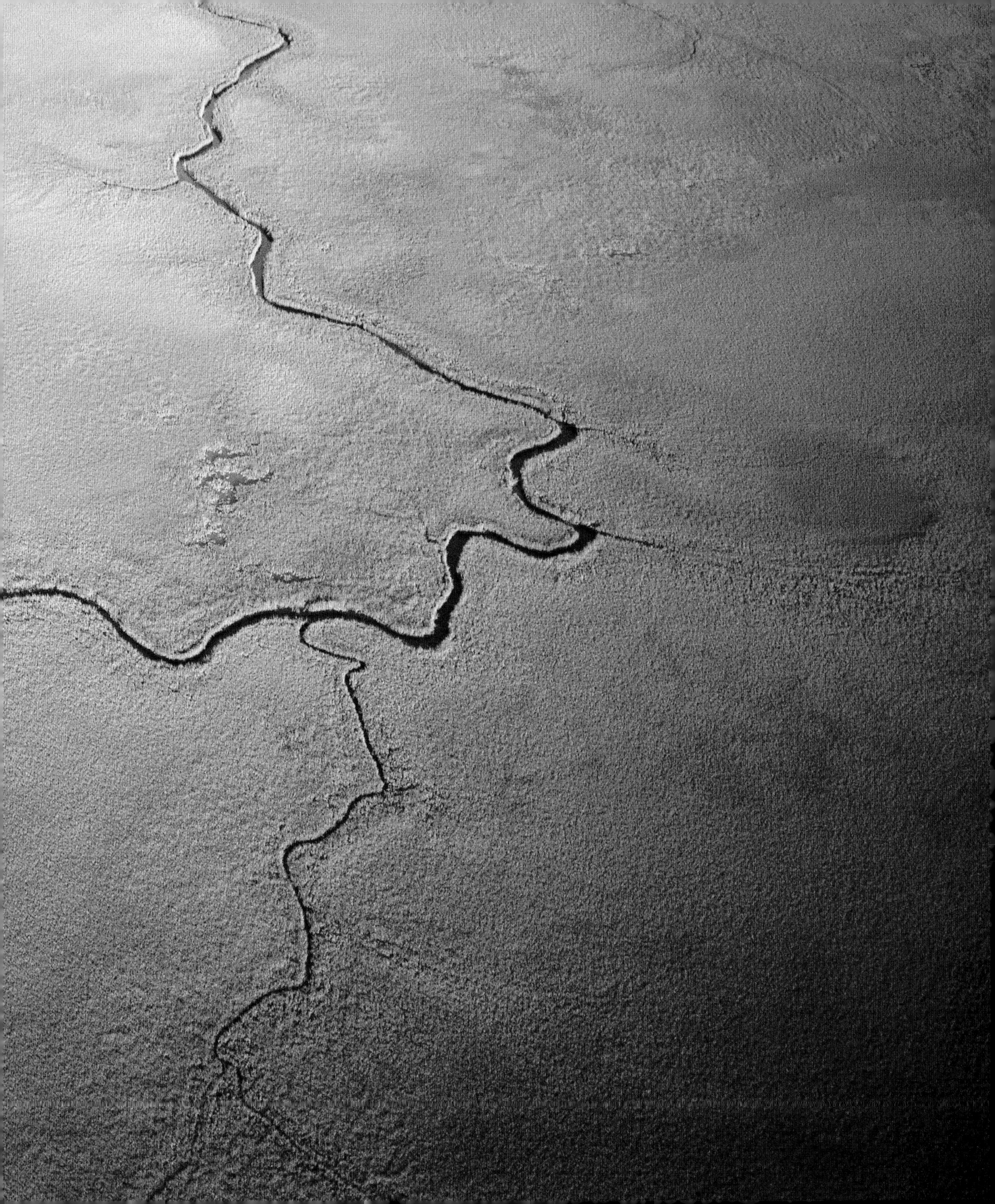

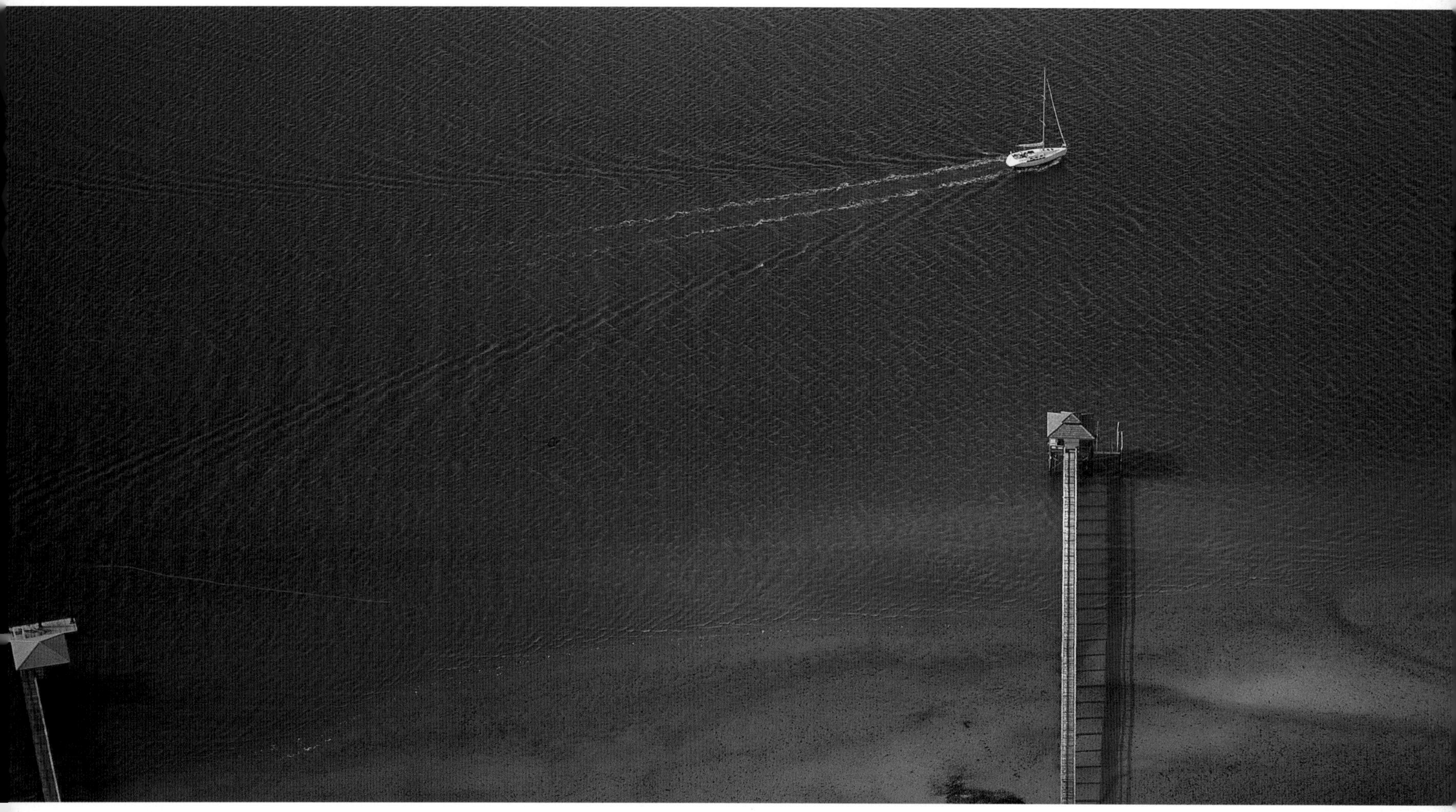

Above: Yacht and boat docks. Hilton Head Island.

Right: Brams Point Road and Broad Creek. Beaufort County.

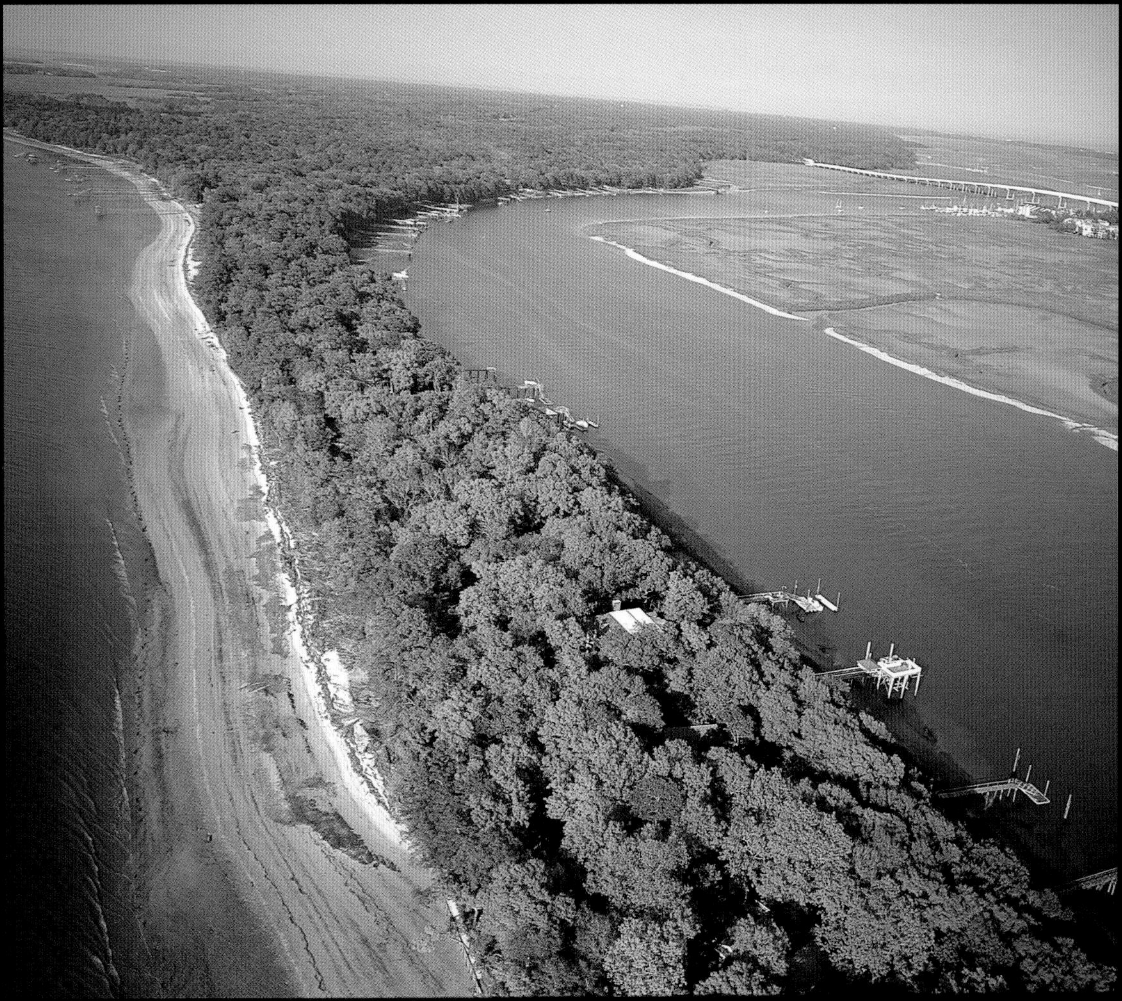

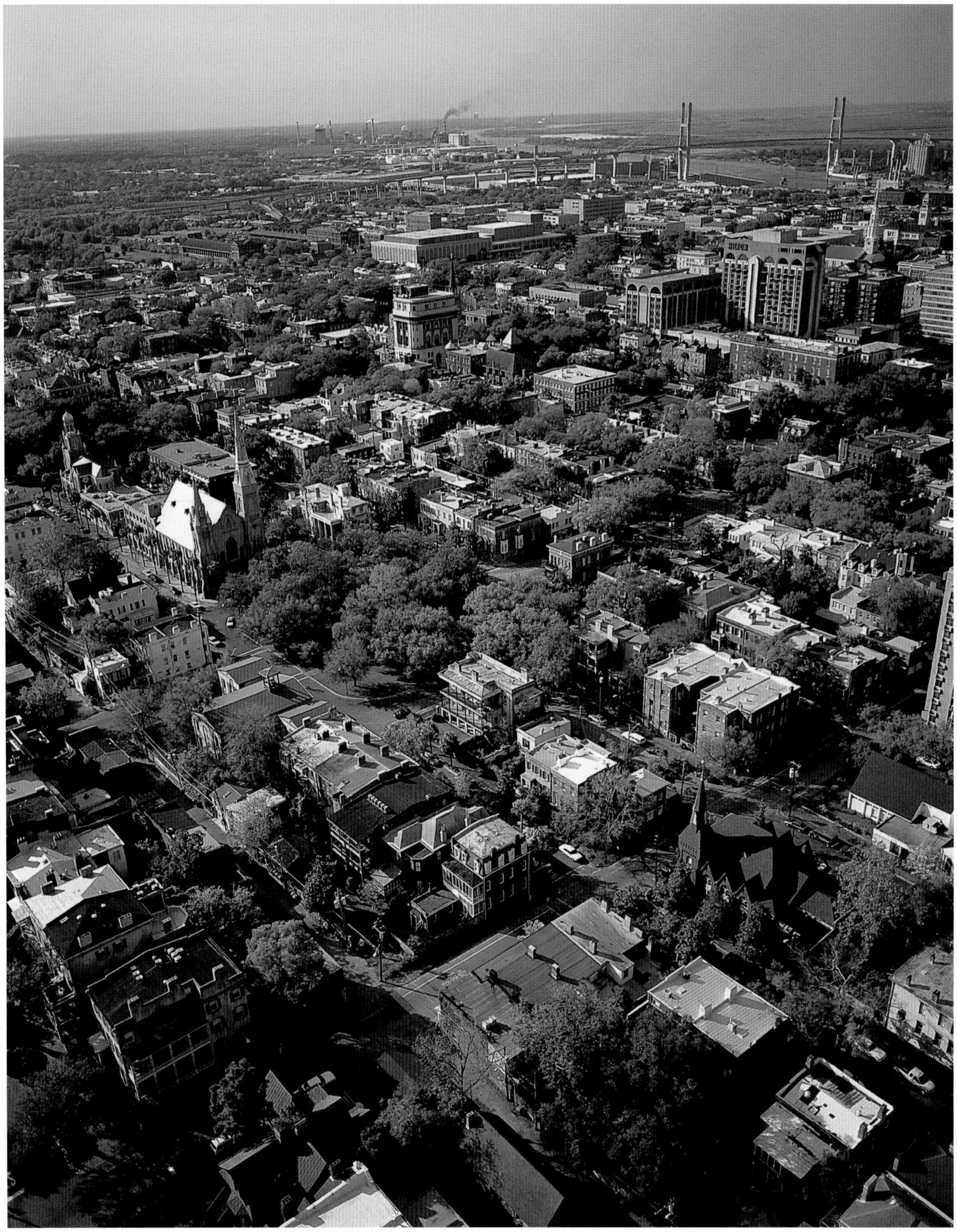

Above: Savannah with Talmadge Memorial Bridge in the background.

Right: Near Fripp Island.

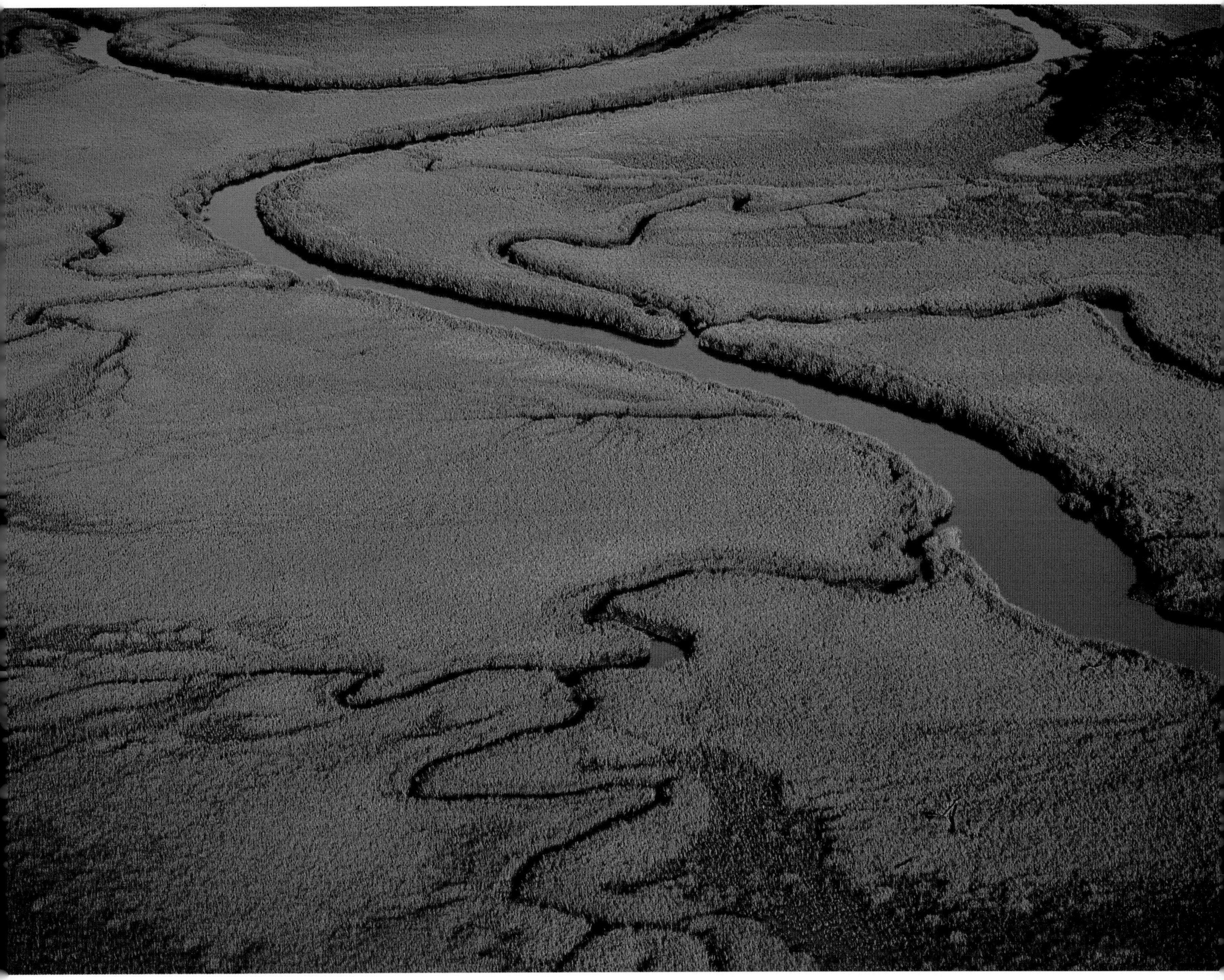

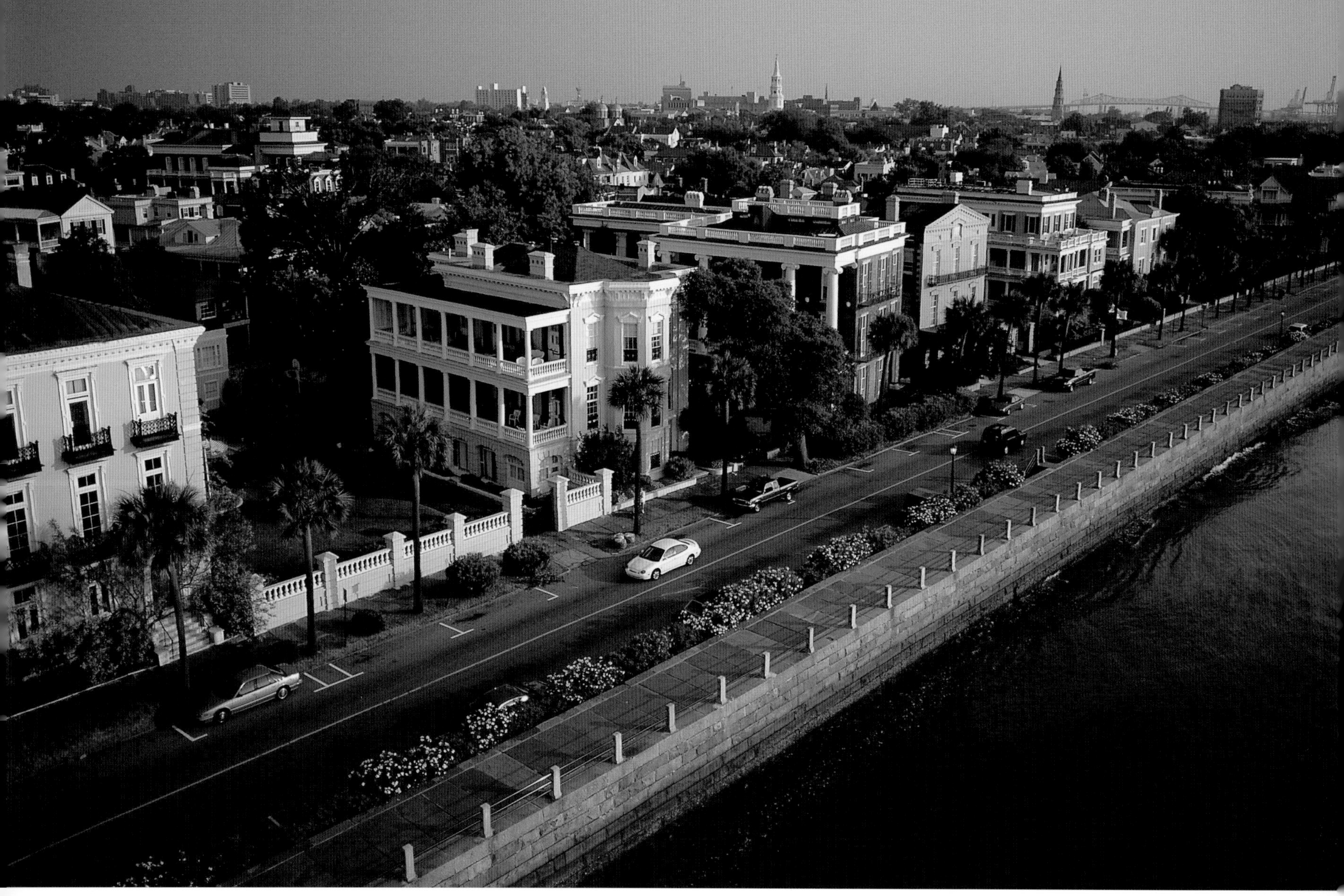

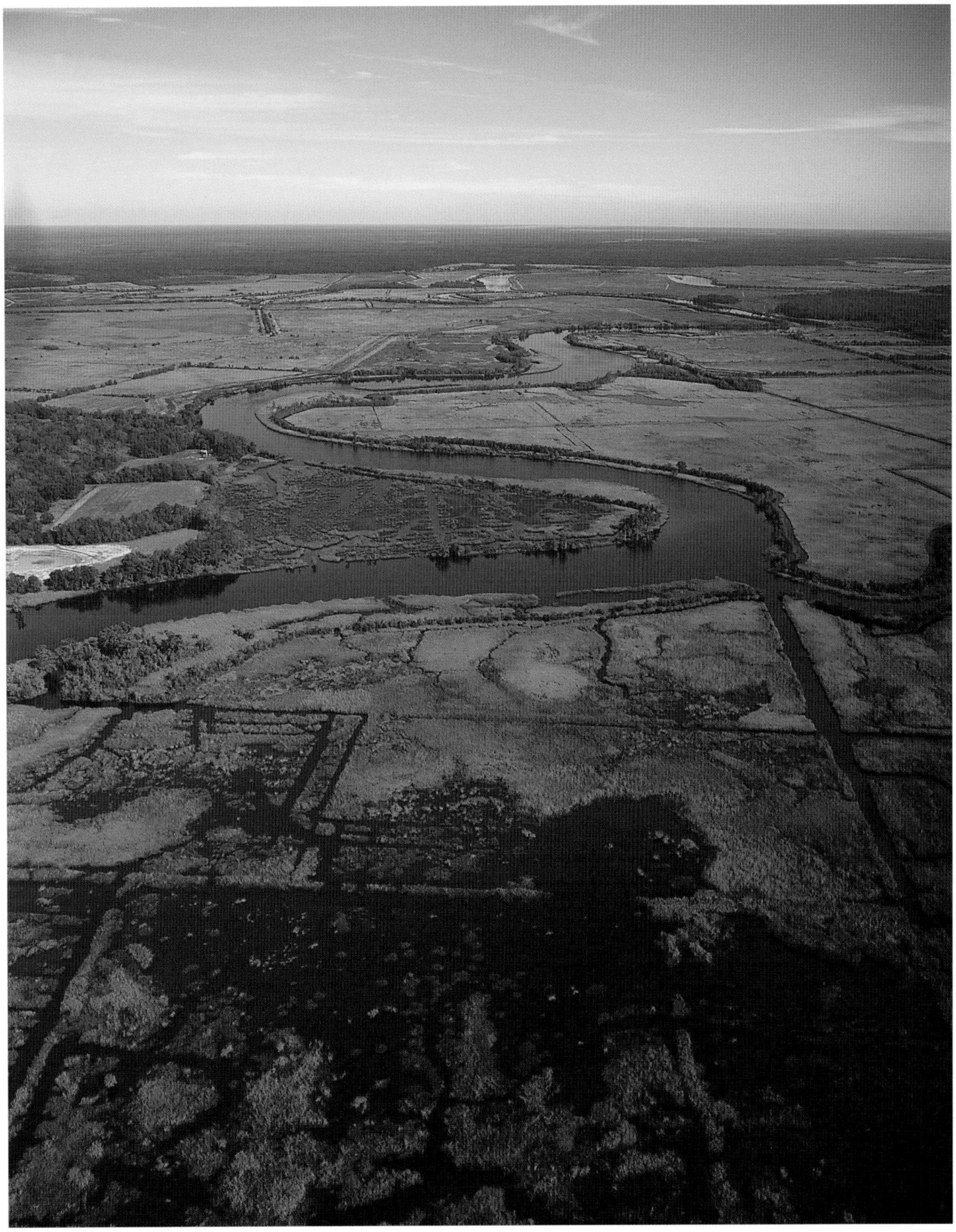

Above: Former rice fields. ACE Basin.

Left: Houses along the Battery. Charleston.

Next Page: Jets at Marine Corps Air Station. Beaufort.

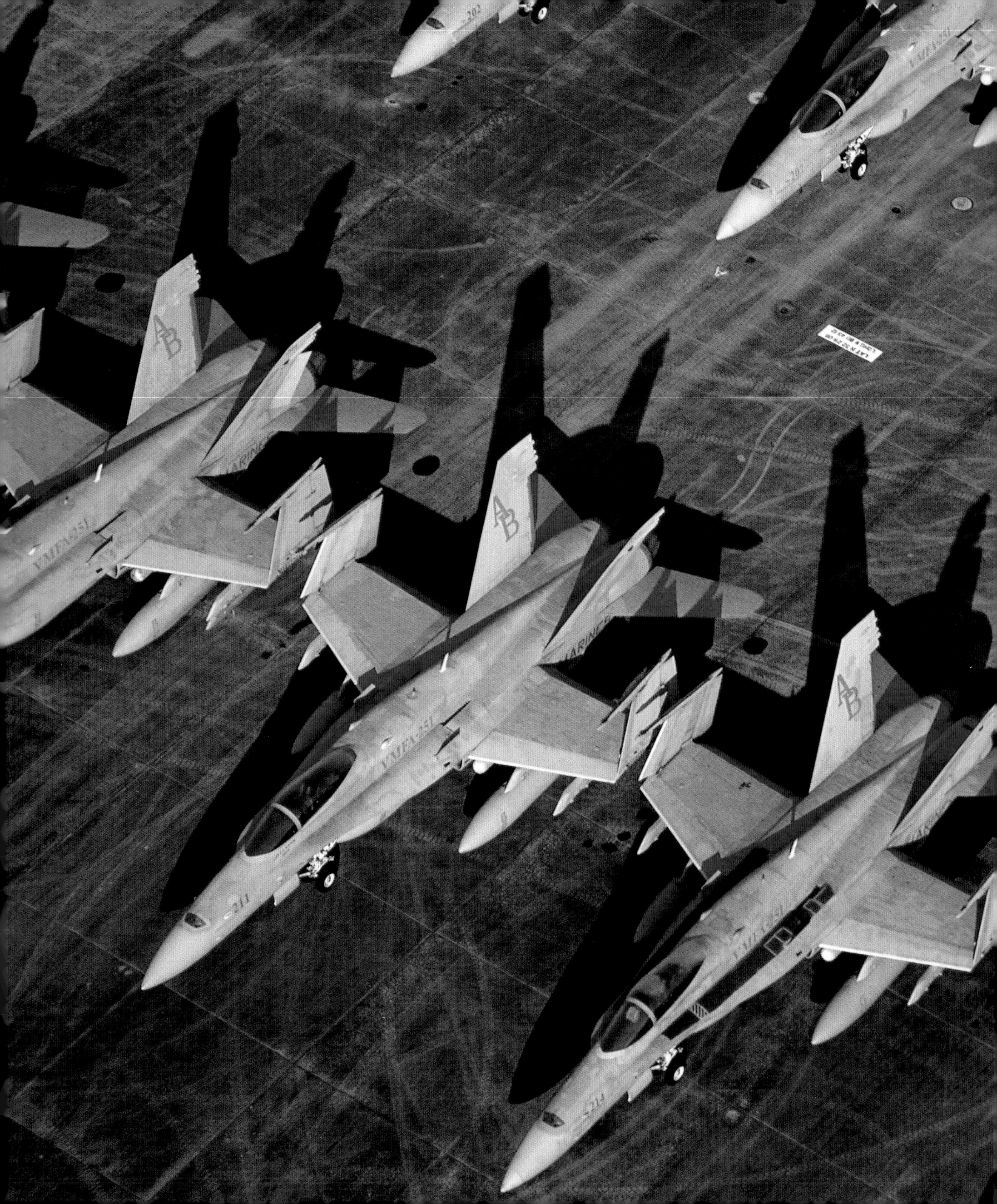
AB
VMFA-251
211
214

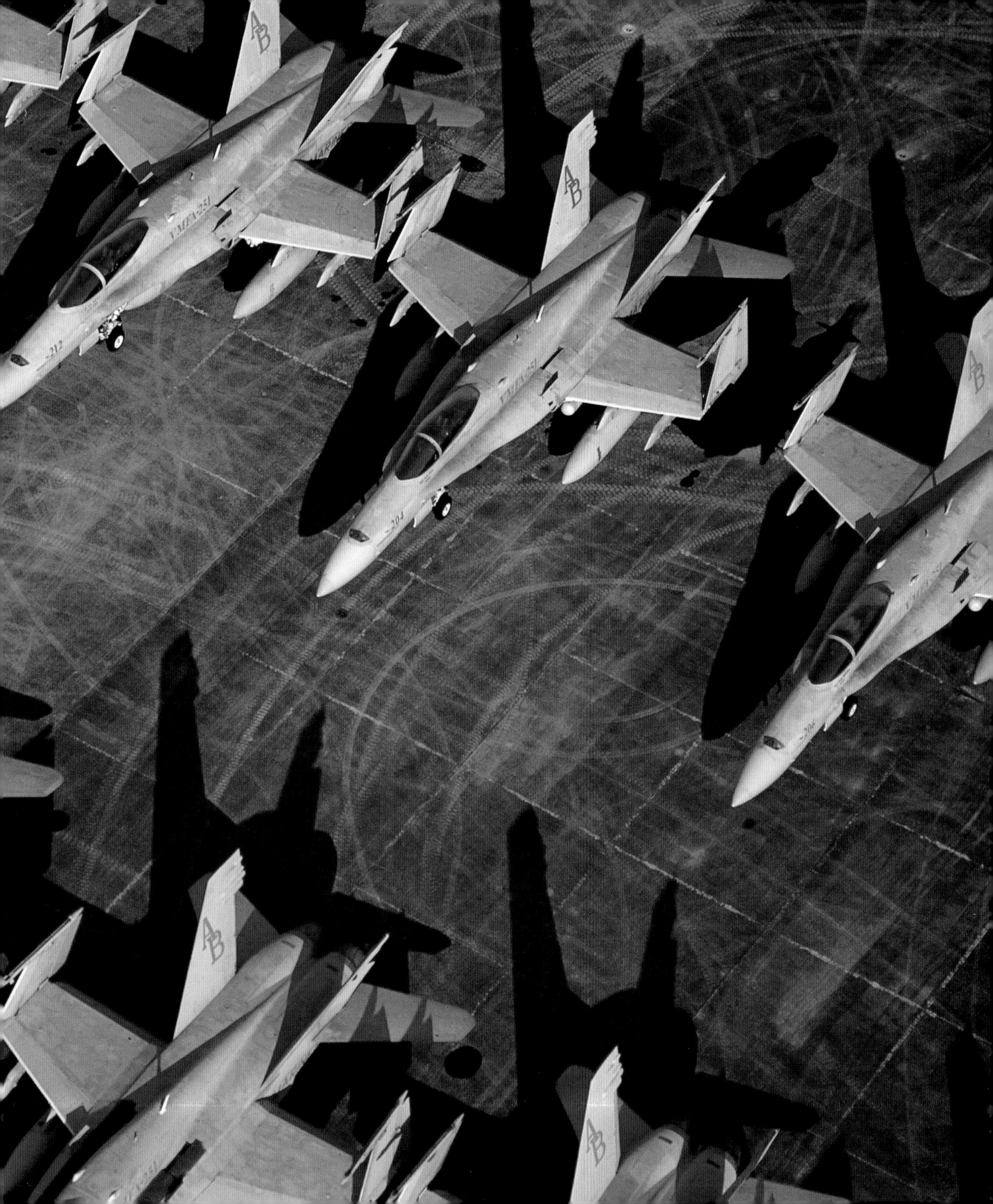
AB
VMFA-251
212
204
206

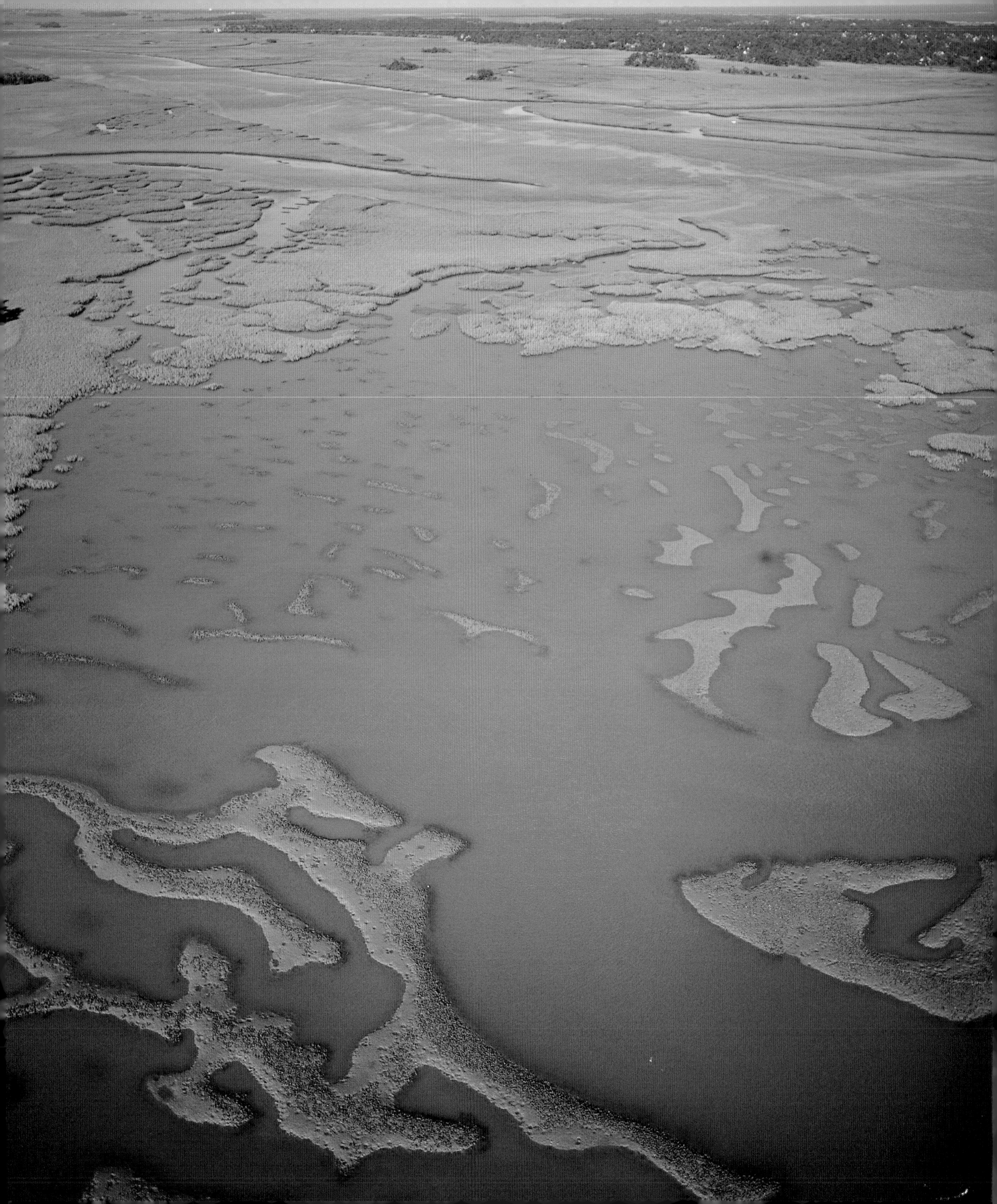

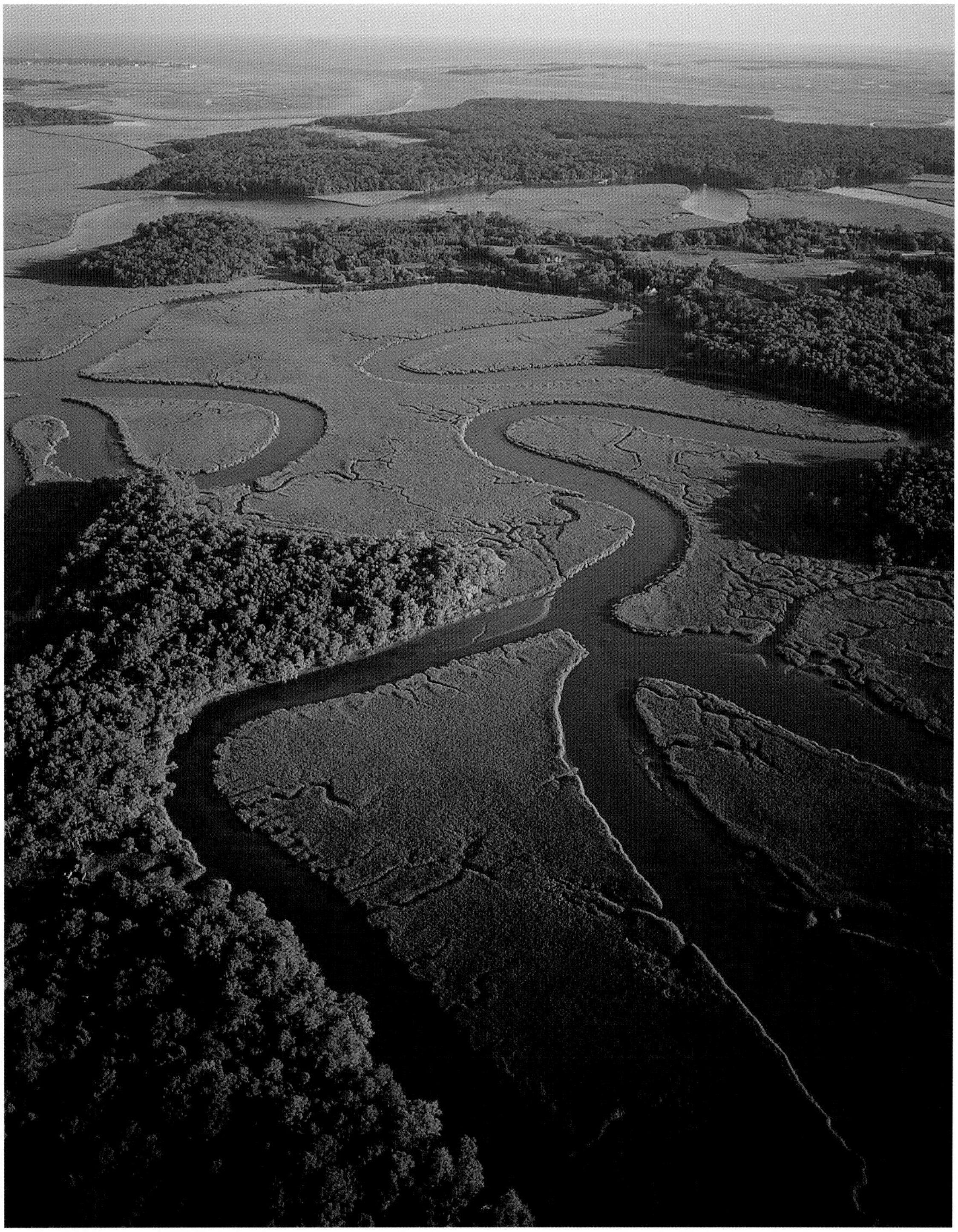

Above: Near Edisto Island.

Left: Tidal flats near Johns Island.

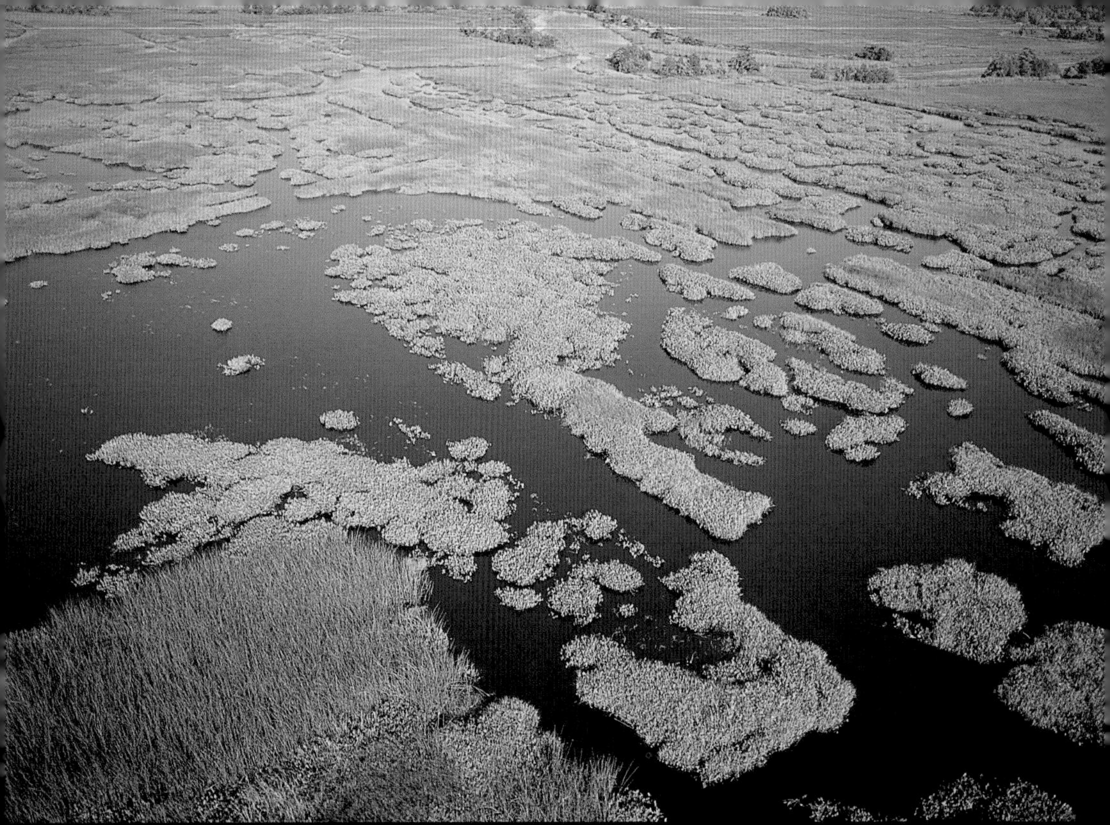

Above: Old rice fields at Combahee River.

Right: ACE Basin.

Next Page: Daufuskie Island along the Cooper River

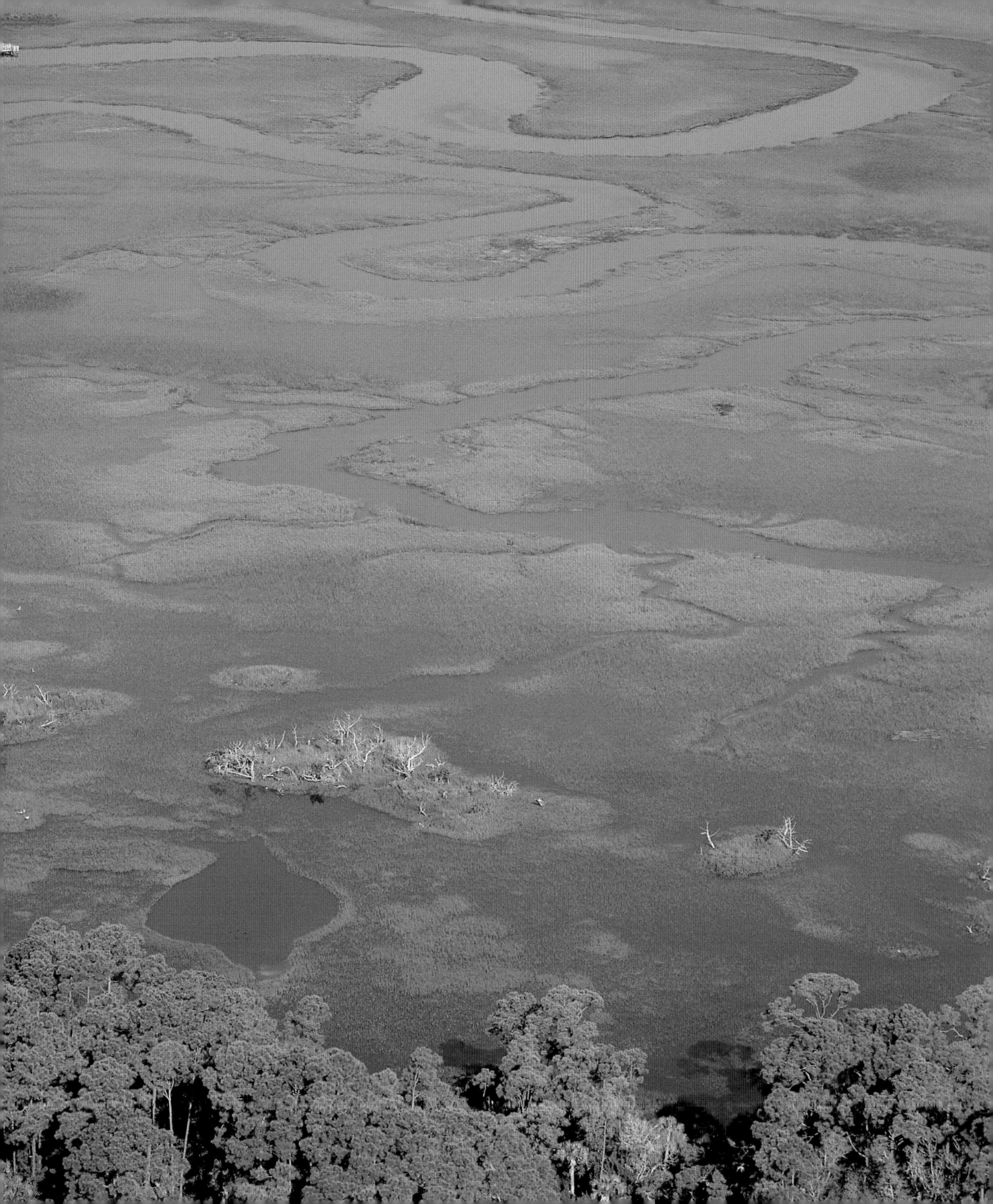

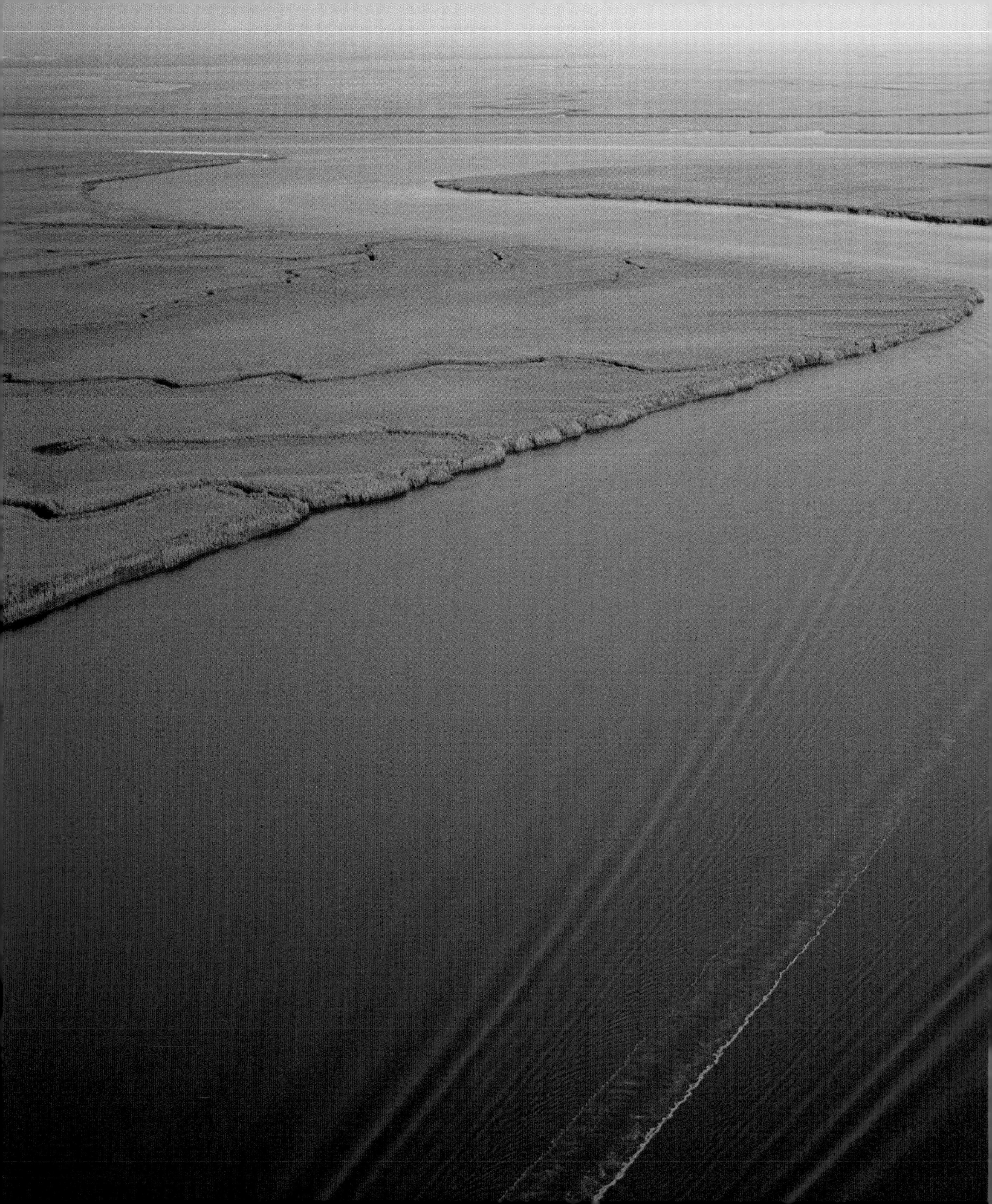

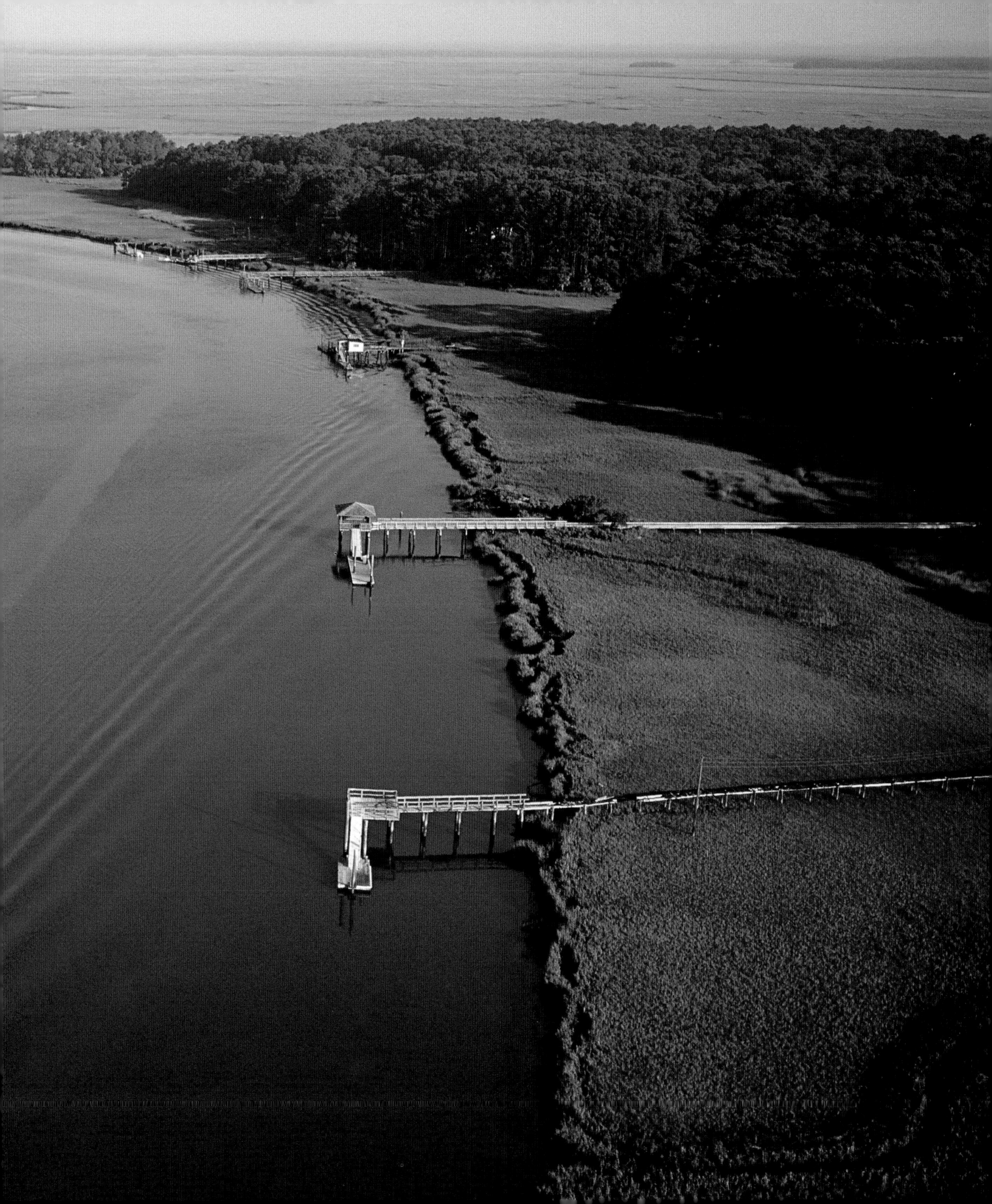

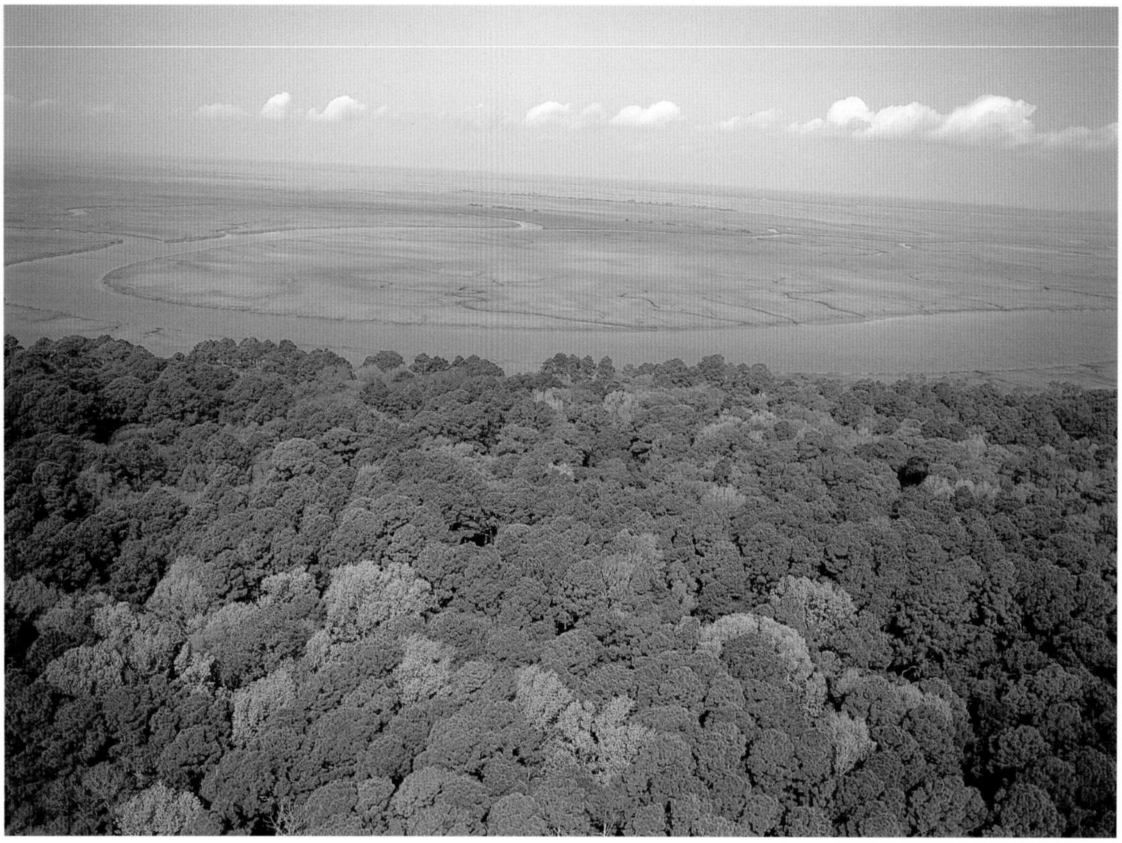

Above: Hunting Island looking across to Harbor Island.

Right: Morris Island Lighthouse.

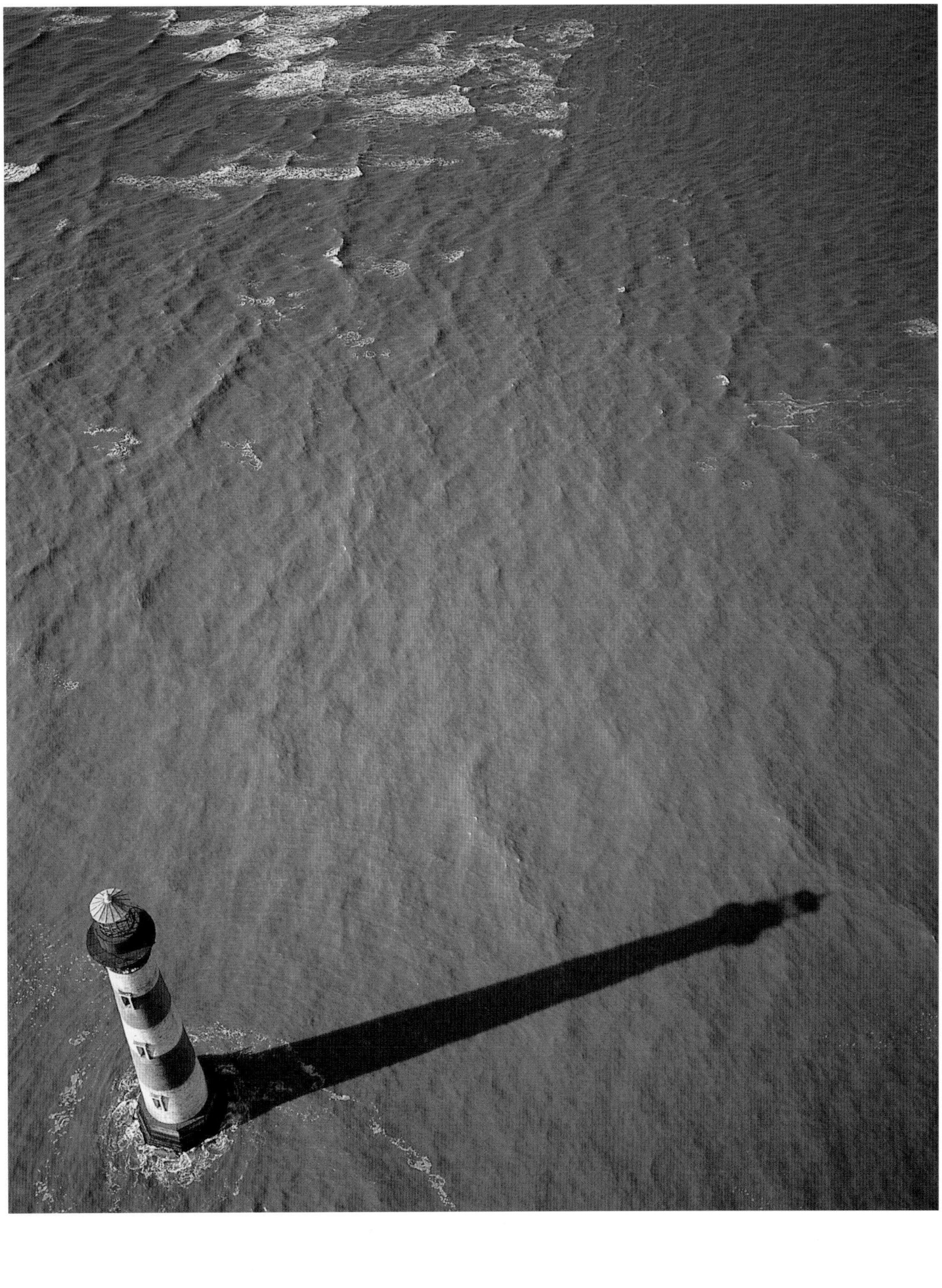

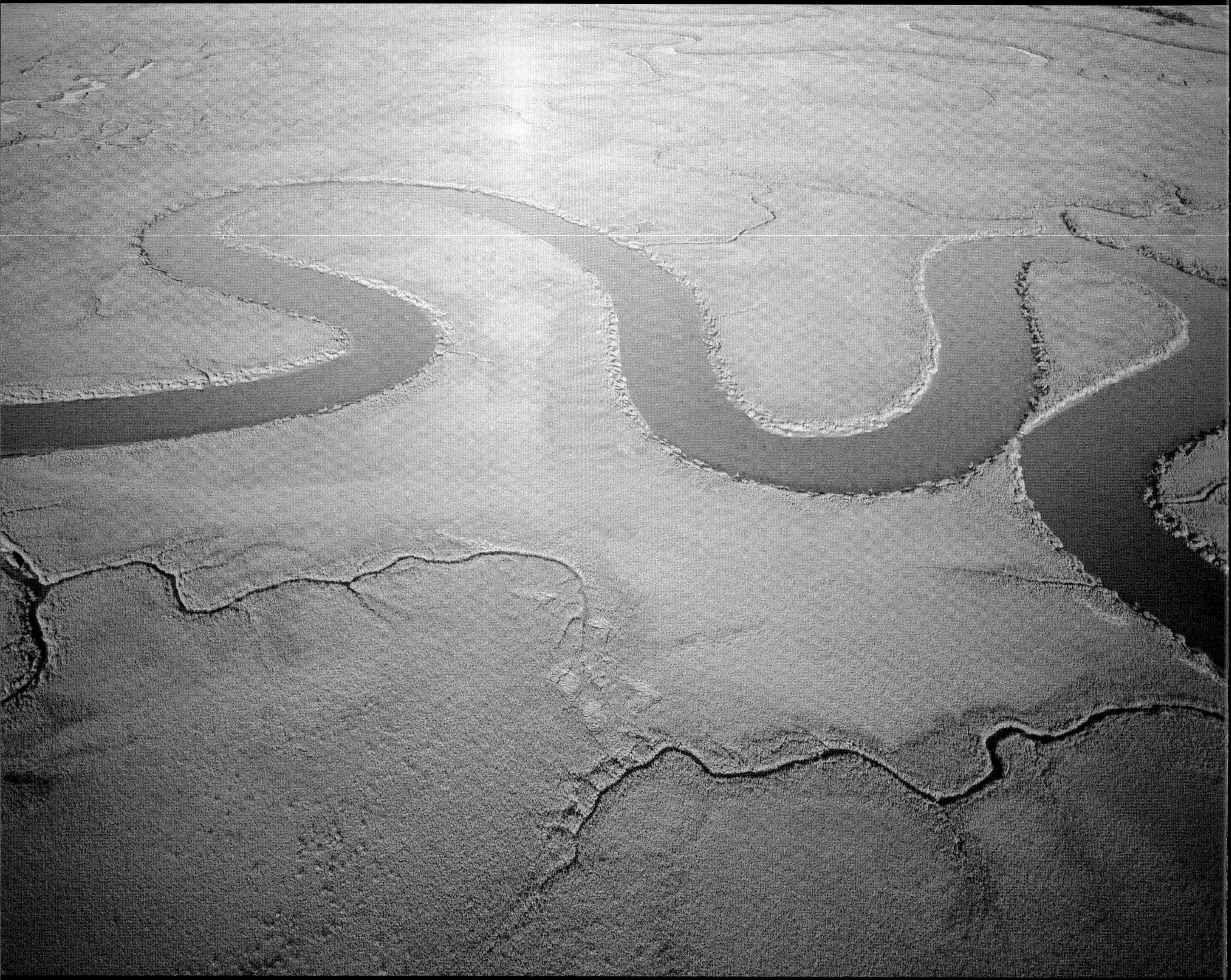

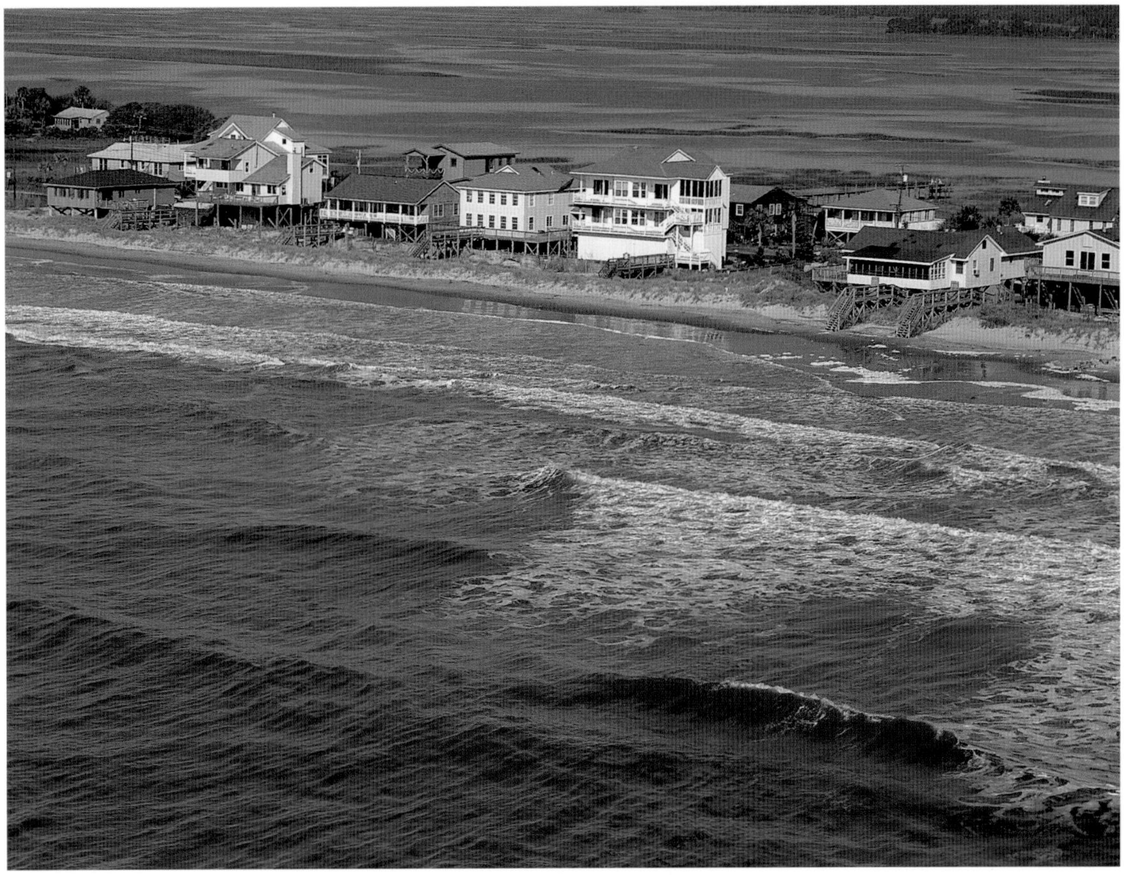

Above: Ashley Avenue at Folly Beach.

Left: Patterns of waterways. St. Helena Island.

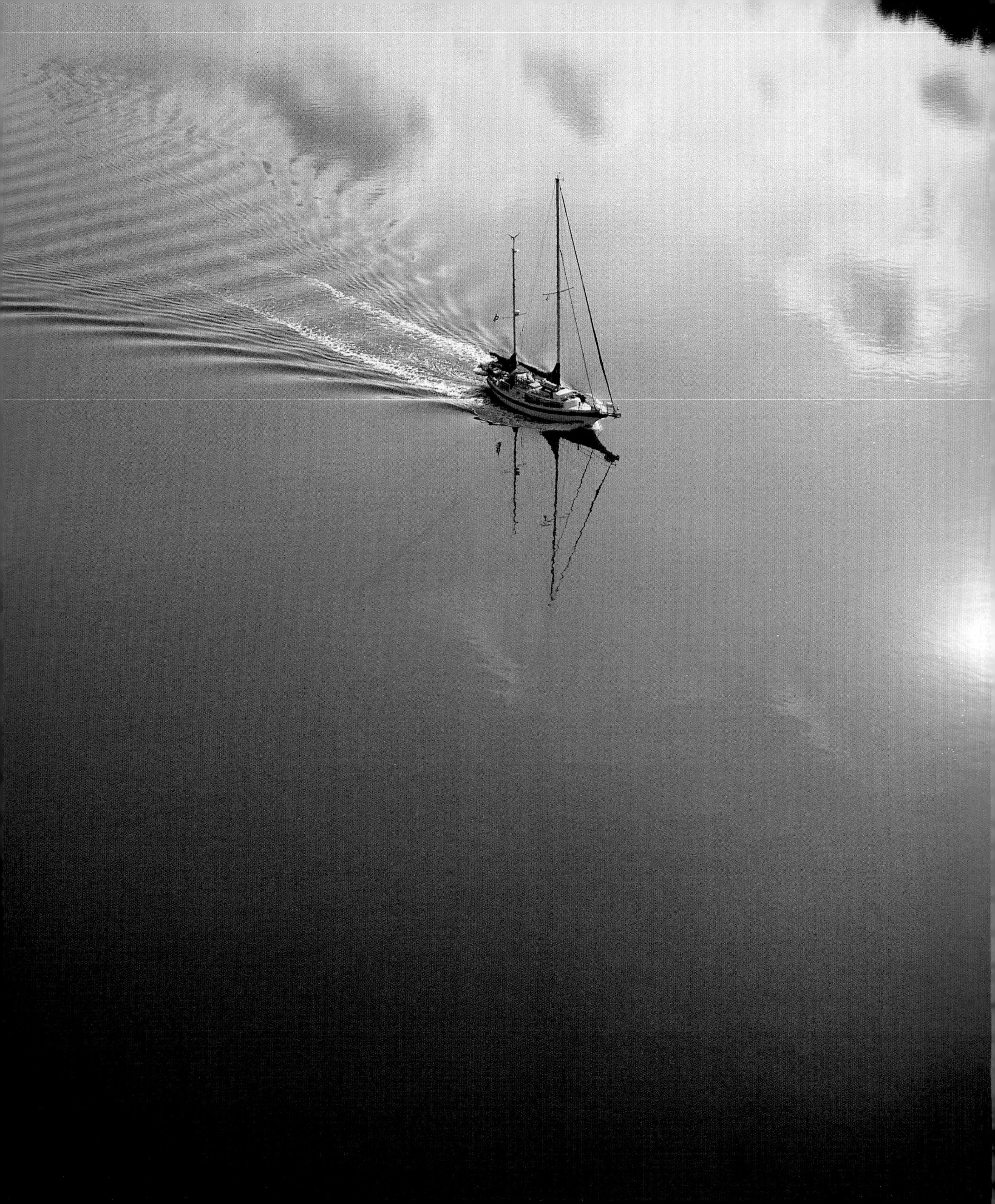

Left: Yacht and reflections of clouds, Beaufort River

To my beautiful wife, Adele. I'll always love you.

Jason

Jason Hawkes has specialized in aerial photography for twelve years, and published eighteen books, including titles on London, Britain, Ireland and Provence. He is based in London and works around Europe and the United States for publishing, advertising and design clients. His photographs have won awards from Association of Photographers, Campaign and D&AD. Hawkes runs a specialists aerial photographic library which can be viewed at www.jasonhawkes.com. He is married to Adele - a media buyer, writer and mother.